HAZARDOUS

TO YOUR

WEALTH

*Extraordinary Popular Delusions
and the Madness of Mutual Fund Experts*

Robert Markman

ELTON-WOLF PUBLISHING

Vancouver • Seattle • Denver • Milwaukee • Portland

Library of Congress Catalog Number: 99-68494
ISBN: 1-58619-006-7

10 9 8 7 6 5 4 3 2 1

First Printing: January 2000
Printed in the United States of America

Designed and typeset
by Gopa Design

Published by Elton-Wolf Publishing
1101 Alaskan Way, Pier 55, Suite 301
Seattle, WA 98101
206-748-0345
E-mail: info@elton-wolf.com
Internet: http://www.elton-wolf.com
Seattle • Vancouver • Los Angeles
Milwaukee • Denver • Portland

HAZARDOUS TO YOUR WEALTH

This book is dedicated to the clients of Markman Capital.

Table of Contents

PART TWO:
A RETURN TO SANITY

Acknowledgments

I AM A MOST FORTUNATE MAN. I am blessed with an abundance of caring, smart, generous and energetic people in my life, without whom I could never have attempted to write this book. The greatest and most pleasurable act involved in this project is to indulge myself by formally naming and thanking them.

Everyone at Markman Capital Management shares credit for whatever value this book possesses. Over the past year each has worked hard to create an environment that would allow me to carve out the time and space to think and write. Now that they've seen how little I am really needed around the office, they must surely be asking what I'm going to do once the book is completed.

Of the Markman Capital staff, three in particular must be singled out: Phil Montville, Rick London, and Judith Fansler. Phil works side by side with me every day researching funds and helping to analyze the myriad of economic details that impact on their performance. Rick has been a multitalented rock of support, stepping in to provide invaluable assistance in a variety of areas. From his work on specialized research projects to his yeoman-like efforts to clean up and clarify my often garbled, "Greenspeak"-like writing, he has been an invaluable colleague. Judith is the glue that holds Markman Capital together. She has made sure that, with all the distractions the writing of this book threw before us, we remained focused on what has always been job number one: doing the best job we can for our clients every day. If this book resonates with the typical investor, it's largely because Judith had the courage to tell her boss on many occasions that what he had written was "just not right yet."

Beth Chapman is the Queen of all Media Relations. No one is better at "getting the story out." I am deeply indebted to her not only for expanding my horizons but also for suggesting this book in the first place. In both my writing and speaking, she has helped me become a better communicator.

This book is dedicated to all the clients of Markman Capital, but two, in particular, deserve special acknowledgment. The late Robert Peller, during the time I had the pleasure of working with him, helped me grow in many ways. He was quite gifted and would regularly challenge me in ways that served to clarify and focus my investing process. I miss him very much. It's probably not very professional to admit this, but Jim Henrich is my most important client. Not because he's the largest (he isn't). Not because he was Markman Capital's first client (though he was.) And not because he has always been the easiest to get along with (he hasn't been). Jim, from the very beginning, understood what we were trying to create better than anyone else I've ever worked with. His faith and constancy, even during times when the results in his account did not support it, have touched all of us at Markman Capital. Through the years, Jim has been a remarkable "early warning signal." He seemed to sense both the good and the bad long before other clients, and often well before we in the office realized what the score was. We all learned long ago to heed his advice, even when his conclusions make us uncomfortable; he's almost always right. Thanks, Jim, for caring.

The last and biggest thank you goes to my wife Emilee and

my daughters Allie and Katie who, with unquestioning good nature and love, put up with my distractions and preoccupations in the writing of this book. None of this would have been possible without the deep support and encouragement Emilee has always abundantly given. Her insightful opinions about people's needs and motivations are so canny as to be uncanny. What I have learned from her has helped me be in the world in a way which has allowed these investment ideas to see the light of day. As if that's not enough, she always seems to find the typo that six previous proofreaders have missed.

I must disclose that there are some parts of this book that are the sole result of my efforts, credit for which I cannot share with anyone else. They are the errors, for which I am solely responsible.

PREFACE

"The great menace to progress is not ignorance,
but the illusion of knowledge."
Daniel Boorstin, historian

THE CONVENTIONAL WISDOM in the mutual fund world may be conventional, but it's not wisdom. All the fancy charts, arcane terminology, and pseudo-scientific research can't hide one uncomfortable fact: The "smart money"—the experts—have been turning in crummy results for some time.

Followers of conventional wisdom have hit into the investment equivalent of a double play. They've lagged the market when it's gone up, but haven't achieved an offsetting stability on the downside.

This book takes a skeptical look at what, until now, has been the commonly accepted way of things in the mutual fund world. You'll see that much of what financial planners, the media, advisors and mutual fund companies have told you is simply not true. It's a bizarre, almost Alice in Wonderland type story. We'll see how efforts to reduce risk can actually become dangerous, while attempts to achieve large gains can result in loss, not profits. It's a story of mutual fund expertise gone mad, all the while proclaiming itself as the epitome of rationality.

The good news is that by shining a light on the delusions that keep your portfolio from its fullest potential, we will be able to see more clearly what actually does work. You'll find to your amazement—or anger—that what works is much different from what you've always been advised to do.

I wrote this book for the informed general investor, one who brings more common sense to the table than technical knowledge. I have tried to reduce, and in most cases eliminate, the usual investment jargon that clutters so many money books. Financial service professionals too often assume that "lay people" possess the same specialized vocabulary and shorthand as they do. It's been my experience that many intelligent and successful nonfinancial people have a hard time giving accurate definitions of even basic investment terms like PE's, asset allocation, and bid/ask prices. If that's you, don't worry. When the need arises to use industry lingo, I'll assume nothing and try to provide clear definitions and perspectives to ensure that we're all talking about the same thing.

As Victor Hugo wrote, *"There is nothing so powerful as an idea whose time has come."* The time has come to reevaluate the accumulated dogma of the mutual fund world. I guarantee that after reading this book, you will never approach your investments the same way again.

INTRODUCTION

"When someone persuades me that I am wrong, I change my mind. What do you do?"
John Maynard Keynes

I AM AN INVESTMENT ADVISOR and my firm, Markman Capital Management, constructs and manages diversified no-load portfolios for investors who choose not to do it themselves. Some industry observers would contend that most folks could do this themselves, and that paying someone else a fee of 1% or so per year to do this is wasteful. "Why not," they say, "just do it yourself?" Good point. Unlike most of my peers in the industry, I believe that many investors can and *should* do it themselves.

I am also a realist and know that the "do it yourself" route is simply not practical for a number of investors. There are a lot of intelligent people who don't feel they have the time or resources to do it well on their own. They are among the many who have decided to use the services of a professional advisor. They expect, not unreasonably, that these professionals should do better than they would themselves. For some, it's not just a matter of getting superior investment performance. They think of the advisor as an "insurance policy." They pay their advisory fee gladly, feeling that if left to their own devices they might make a ghastly mistake with their portfolio, one that could do serious long-term harm. It's a sobering responsibility for advisors like us.

We money managers tend to be a collegial group of people. We're all too aware that the financial markets manage to do a good job of embarrassing and humbling most of us on a regular basis; the last thing we need is one of our peers throwing poison darts in our direction. There's a genuine "live and let live" culture that makes most investment professionals shy away from criticizing others, even when that criticism is well warranted. So I must confess that I was more than a little uncomfortable to write some of the things you'll read in this book. The unavoidable consequence of the material presented here is to call into question the motives, intelligence and judgment of the majority of the folks who labor in the mutual fund world.

My criticism of the industry, however, should not by any means be construed as an intimation of my superiority. Indeed, I couldn't have written this book if I hadn't made all these same mistakes—and more—myself. Just about every myth I expose, every technique I show to be dangerous, every bit of conventional wisdom I shoot holes in, I too believed in and practiced diligently at various times.

I began working in the mutual fund world in 1981 and in 1988 started offering money management services to clients on a fee basis using no-load funds. Markman Capital Management was incorporated in 1990 and is now one of the country's largest, private independent fund advisors, managing over $500 million. The returns we have generated for our clients—as measured by the audited, after fee and expense numbers of the publicly available Markman MultiFunds—are at, or close to, the best in the industry. *(Full disclosure of the performance data of the Markman MultiFunds, with relevant comparisons, can be found in the Appendix.)*

Like all money managers, we have had our good years and our

not so good years. As time passed, however, I began to grow increasingly uncomfortable with how we were executing our fiduciary responsibilities. I felt my team and I were better—smarter—than our results would indicate. There were just too many times when results did not match expectations. Investments that were supposed to provide upside potential ended up dead in the water; funds that were touted as conservative and stable ended up *adding to* portfolio volatility. This seemed to be occurring too many times to be chalked up to the normal vagaries of the markets. I was frustrated; clients were disappointed. As my concern grew, I looked everywhere for answers. Was the market to blame? Although that might sound as effective as blaming the weather, you'd be surprised how many intelligent observers make a living claiming they are not wrong; it's just the market that is so screwy.

Perhaps I could, like some of my peers, blame the clients themselves! Incredible and offensive as this might sound, advisors exist who, rather than confront their own faults, accuse clients of "unreasonable expectations." (As if wanting to participate in the greatest bull market of our lifetimes is an unreasonable expectation.) We rejected this as an absurd "blame the victim" strategy. Or maybe the problem was just *me*. Maybe the Peter Principle had caught up with me, and I'd finally risen to my ultimate level of mediocrity. Fortunately, I could see that many of my experienced and respected peers in the business were doing even worse than I was. If I was mediocre, they were downright dangerous! Since that, too, did not seem to be a reasonable explanation, I could only conclude (with relief!) that I, personally, was not the problem.

As I surveyed the advisor landscape, I could see that, while the details might differ somewhat, the through line was the same:

clients were simply not participating in the great bull market of the '90s. The conventional explanation was that we advisors were erring on the side of caution and that when the markets got rocky, our techniques would pay off. Then the markets called our bluff: they got rocky *and the techniques didn't pay off.* This was not just an isolated event. We saw it happen time after time over the past ten years. Lag on the upside, yet still get hurt on the downside. This was no way to run a railroad.

At professional conferences, in individual conversations, in industry journals, I heard this same story repeated time after time. *Everyone* was screwing up! Most strange. How could everyone be executing so incompetently at the same time? Professional investment advisors are an intelligent and successful group of folks. Given their differing styles, personalities and techniques, it seemed statistically improbable that they were all bungling simultaneously. The only possible answer was intriguing: *Perhaps the system itself was flawed?* Maybe that's why so many advisors, from Maine to California, were experiencing variations on the same troublesome theme. We were all drinking from the same poisoned well. Was that really the problem? Were we caught in a closed loop of failure, with results diminishing ever more as we executed what we had been taught?

Since the first step in finding a solution is to correctly identify the problem, I went to work researching how the industry was executing the investment process. My staff and I embarked on a top-to-bottom review of what we were doing and why we were doing it. We assumed nothing. We examined our tactics and strategies and re-researched all of the accumulated "wisdom" that over the years we had begun to take for granted. We removed the intellectual autopilot and searched for proof of what seemed to have become quasi-religious dogma.

Stripping away years of mental varnish was not fun. Especially when we found that underneath the varnish was not the elegant investment model we thought we were working with. We found, much to our chagrin, that there was *not* proof for many of the accepted concepts in which we had always believed. The dogma sounded like it *should* work, but the facts to support it simply didn't exist. The evidence forced us to conclude that:

◆ Diversifying among multiple asset classes is doomed to failure.

◆ The magic tools of Modern Portfolio Theory and Efficient Frontiers are useless at best and dangerous at worst.

◆ The conventional wisdom that small companies outperform large companies is false.

◆ The conventional wisdom that international investments can help reduce risk and increase return is false.

◆ The industry confuses volatility with risk, thus leading investors to make short-term decisions in a long-term program.

◆ The obsession of the media and many investment professionals with short-term events and results creates an unhealthy imperative to make short-term tactical moves often at the expense of long-term performance.

Holy mackerel, we thought, it's all a bunch of baloney! A trillion-dollar industry was nothing less than an intellectual Rube Goldberg machine, built on half truths, incorrect interpretations, flawed data, unrealistic expectations and absurd contradictions. The more "state-of-the-art" the execution, the worse the results. There was clearly something rotten in the state-of-the-art. It was no wonder that portfolios based on accepted doctrine did not produce the results intended!

So, what to do? We could sew the patient back up, so to speak, pretend we didn't see what we saw, and go on as before. At least we would have company in our mediocrity—everyone else seemed to be doing the same thing. (It's been remarked that many would rather fail in a group than risk succeeding alone. Very true, at least in the investment world.) Alternatively, we could, armed with our new insights, go back to the drawing board and try to construct a way of meeting—or exceeding—our clients' expectations, with a strategy and methodology that would actually be supported by real-world evidence. We chose the latter, and we think we've succeeded. You're holding the proof in your hands.

As you read this book, I urge you to resist the temptation to discount our argument when it becomes too painful to accept. It won't be easy reading how you may have wasted the last 5–10 years. In my discussions with advisors and journalists, I have often come away amazed at what some people will say and do so as not to confront change. This book is a head-on assault on the most sacred cows in the mutual fund world. I expect the response to be furious to the point of hysteria. All I can say, and all I hope you will keep in mind, is what Ronald Reagan said: "Facts are stubborn things." It's not me, but the facts that will kill the sacred cows of the mutual fund world.

PART ONE

MADNESS AND DELUSIONS

CHAPTER ONE

WHEN THE SOLUTION BECOMES THE PROBLEM: ASSET ALLOCATION AND DIVERSIFICATION

"There is no sadder sight in the world than to see a beautiful theory killed by a brutal fact."
Thomas H. Huxley

ASSET ALLOCATION and diversification—the foundation concepts of mutual fund investing—are, ironically, the source of the industry's dysfunction. The very same ideas that were supposed to help mutual fund investors have, in fact, created enormous obstacles to successful portfolio management. Over the past year, as I floated a few trial balloons on this topic among selected advisors and journalists, I got the feeling that I had touched the "third rail" of the investment world. Criticize asset allocation and diversification? I might as well take potshots at Mom and apple pie. I was committing the investment equivalent of high treason.

Nevertheless, asset allocation and diversification, in the form most often promoted by the industry, is a good idea gone dangerously out of control. What began as simple, common sense, achievable approaches to portfolio building have been hijacked by those who are more interested in promoting academic theories than getting superior results in the real world. These worthy concepts have been taken far beyond reason, creating a quagmire that the industry can't seem to escape. As we'll soon see, the misuse of asset allocation and diversification can put your entire investment program in jeopardy.

ASSET ALLOCATION, DIVERSIFICATION AND THE URGE TO BE SAFE

Risk. The assumption of risk, the avoidance of risk, the rewards of risk, the perils of risk—these are powerful forces driving our investment experience. Indeed, the entire structure of portfolio management is built to accommodate methods of defining and dealing with risk.

A portfolio of just one stock could be very risky; if that one company does poorly, you have nothing to fall back on. To reduce that risk, you buy several stocks on the assumption that if one company falls on hard times, others may be doing well and thus offset your loss. This kind of risk—the risk associated with how a particular company may fare—is called *business risk* (also referred to as unsystematic risk). By selecting an intelligent basket of stocks, you can significantly reduce the business risk in your portfolio. In a classic example, owning the stock of an oil company can reduce the business risk of owning an airline stock. Theoretically, if energy prices go up, negatively impacting the energy dependent airline, the oil company would likely benefit.

The benefits of diversification in a stock portfolio can be felt with the addition of just a few stocks. By the time 12–18 stocks are present, some 90% of the business risk has been eliminated (assuming, of course, that all of the stocks are not within the same industry!).

The other type of risk in your portfolio is called *market risk* (also sometimes referred to as systematic risk). This is the risk associated not with any particular company, but rather *with the market as a whole.* This risk cannot be diversified away by investing in more of the same type of asset because when the market as a whole goes down, *all* stocks will have a tendency to be negatively affected. (Note that with business risk we were worried that a company would not "make it" and could theoretically go out of business, resulting in a permanent loss of capital. With market risk, we are looking at the *volatility* of an investment, not its *viability*.)

Market risk is what most industry experts are referring to when they discuss risk. This way of looking at risk—as a measure of volatility (usually over a fairly short period)—was first introduced over forty years ago by Harry Markowitz. It was Markowitz who laid the groundwork for what we now know as Modern Portfolio Theory. Over time it has become the most widely accepted concept in all of investing. Also the most tyrannical and destructive—and wrong! (Warren Buffet's partner, Charlie Munger, when asked about Modern Portfolio Theory, instantly replied, "Twaddle!" He added that the concepts are "A type of dementia I can't even classify.") In chapter four, we'll revisit risk and volatility and show how linking them together sends you off on the wrong path. For now, though, we'll focus on how Modern Portfolio Theory dictates what you put in your portfolio.

According to Modern Portfolio Theory, to reduce market risk, you must own investments that respond differently to economic conditions. The measurement of how one investment acts relative to another is called its *correlation*. Two investments that react much the same way are said to have positive correlations. If they react in ways that are not all that similar, they have low correlations. If they react in exact opposite ways, they are said to be negatively correlated. And that's where the concept of an *asset class* comes in.

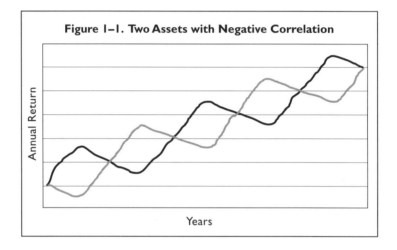

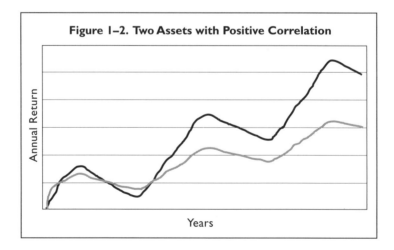

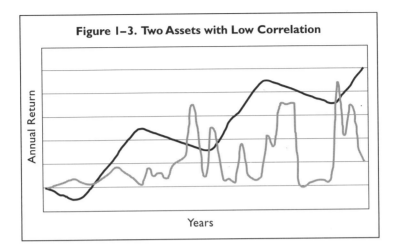

Figure 1–3. Two Assets with Low Correlation

ASSET CLASSES

An asset class is any broad category of investments with similar characteristics and correlations. *Stocks* is an asset class. *Bonds* is an asset class. *Cash* is an asset class. Investors are told to try to achieve a mixture of different asset classes that, due to their low (or negative) correlations, will produce the optimal combination of reward and risk for the portfolio. The classic example is illustrated in Figure 1–1.

This mix and match process is called *asset allocation*. When limited to the broad choices of stocks, bonds, and cash it's a prudent exercise. And if that's all investors did, or advisors advised, or reporters reported, there would be little reason to write this book. Unfortunately the mutual fund world has, over the past 25 years, taken an aggressive—even radical—path regarding asset allocation.

SLICING AND DICING

Over time, investment professionals and academics looked at return data from various investments and concluded that even within the broad asset category of stocks, there were any number of *sub asset classes*. It seemed that many of these sub asset classes exhibited characteristics different from the others; they would rise and fall at different times and at different rates. Some researchers noted that foreign stocks often moved independently of U.S. stocks. Others found that small company stocks exhibited different performance characteristics than large company stocks. Real estate stocks had their own performance dynamic that differed from that of the broad market. Emerging markets, of course, marched to their own drummer. And so on and so on....

This burst of scholarly energy was spurred on by the searing experience of the 1973–74 bear market. During that two-year period, the U.S. market declined some 40%, the most devastating plunge since the Great Depression. Many of the most popular and widely held companies sank even further. For many on Wall Street, the apocalypse had arrived.

Then came the "wild and crazy" financial events of the following half dozen years. Gold, real estate, oil, and small caps experienced frenzied rises in the face of continued blue chip listlessness. All of a sudden, the broad investment community was exposed to a range of highly profitable alternatives that had previously not entered into most investors' calculations.

The coincidental rise of computers, with their data gathering and number crunching power, was all that was needed to give birth to the new paradigm that viewed portfolios in a much more segmented manner. We soon had research that "proved" that small caps outperformed large caps. That foreign stocks hedged the downside risk of U.S. stocks. That emerging markets could not only reduce the volatility of a domestic portfolio, but increase the upside potential as well. That real estate stocks were a low-risk, high-yielding alternative for cautious portfolios. By the late 1980s, the state-of-the-art model called for the equity portion of a fund investor's portfolio to be divided among *several* asset sub classes. No longer would we be held hostage to the fortunes of "the market," as defined by blue chips. We could now choose from a menu of equity sub-asset classes that would help us avoid the pain of being in the wrong place at the wrong time.

Investors, with a wealth of historic data available to them, and computer programs to manipulate the data, could now blend several different asset classes together in a mixture that promised not only to reduce their short-term volatility, but also maintain—if not enhance—their return potential. Advisors could now plot out the return and risk (volatility) patterns of various blends to create a graph that showed investors what their risk/reward trade-off would be with those mixes.

Most of you have seen this inverted Nike-like "swoosh." What is shown is the "*Efficient Frontier.*" Sounds pretty impressive, doesn't it? The efficient frontier purports to show where the maximum level of return lies for any given level of risk.

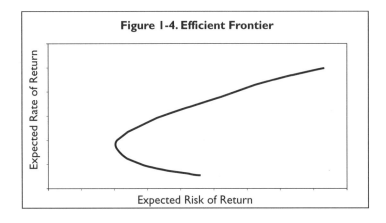

Figure 1-4. Efficient Frontier

To both the untrained observer and the true believer, this process has a scientific tidiness that is awfully hard to resist. It is no wonder that it soon swept the investment world and became the standard by which most knowledgeable and sophisticated practitioners operated. There is only one problem. It is a bogus concept that is intellectually unsupportable. *The efficient frontier simply doesn't exist.* That thousands of intelligent investors have been deluded into believing in the efficacy of diversifying among equity asset classes—a mythical and factually unsupportable construct—is a remarkable example of intellectual mass hysteria.

A DELUSION BASED ON THREE FATAL FLAWS

Diversification and asset allocation, as promoted by the best and the brightest in the mutual fund world, has three fatal flaws (as if one fatal flaw would not be enough!):

1. Reliance on the bankrupt concept of historical correlation.

2. Inability to realize soon enough—if ever—that sometimes things are different.

3. Focus on short-term volatility that causes investment decisions to deteriorate into destructive asset class timing.

THE HISTORIC CORRELATION GAME IS A SHAM

The theory that says you can reduce risk and/or enhance returns by diversifying among different asset classes is based on the belief that we can determine how different investments correlate. In order to mix asset classes together effectively, we have to know what their relative returns and dynamics are likely to be. This can be done only by studying historic returns in an attempt to uncover patterns; we must then assume that those patterns will persist in the future. History and persistency. In order for the efficient frontier to work, you must be right on both counts. Is this possible outside of the academic environment? I suppose it may be possible, but it pays to keep one fact in mind: *It has never been achieved.* It ranks right up there with cold fusion and perpetual motion as a great idea that we've never seen in reality.

The study of historic returns in an attempt to identify patterns is filled with glaring errors. These mistakes are usually the result of two common blunders: Either the data has been misunderstood or the time frame examined has been too short to lead to any useful conclusion.

An example of data misunderstanding is the research that led to the (erroneous) conclusion that small company stocks outperform large company stocks over the long term. This investment old wives' tale is explored in greater depth and exposed for the fraud that it is in the next chapter, "The Small Cap Hoax."

The desire to find correlations that can help investors gain some advantage also leads otherwise intelligent observers to try so hard to spot opportunities that they often jump the gun and make conclusions with far too little data available. One of the most astonishing examples of this (given the renown of those involved) was a claim reported in the June 1996 issue of *Forbes*. The article reported research conducted by Burton Malkiel and J.P. Mei into the efficacy of including emerging market investments in a portfolio. (Malkiel is best known as the author of the influential bestseller, *A Random Walk Down Wall Street*. Mei is an associate professor of finance at New York University.) Their research "proved" that inclusion of emerging markets in a portfolio already diversified in the developed markets of America, Europe and the Far East would *increase your return and reduce your risk*. As *Forbes* reported, "Malkiel and Mei tested their theory over the years 1985 to 1995..." The first thing that would strike any experienced investor reading this article is the absurdity of propounding a strategy that had been tested using *only ten years of data*. That *Forbes*, which prides itself on its hardnosed, iconoclastic stance, would report this outlandish conclusion with nary a skeptical comment is equally bizarre.

Of course, as the investment fates would have it, the results of heeding this ill-thought-out advice were devastating. In the subsequent three years, the average emerging market fund had an abysmal total return of -5.8%. This blunder by one as experienced and respected as Burton Malkiel is an example of how intelligent investors have been blinded to reality and common sense when looking at international investments. In the chapter on foreign investing, "How to Disappoint Yourself in Twelve

Different Languages," we'll show conclusively that whatever the future may hold, there has never been any substantial long-term evidence that foreign investing increases returns or reduces volatility.

We simply do not know how asset classes will act relative to each other in the future. Sure, your financial planner can produce charts and graphs showing how one investment will offset the risks of another, or how one has risen while another has declined, but don't be fooled. All you are seeing is random data forced into patterns that have little or no predictive value. John Rekenthaler, Director of Research at Morningstar, wrote in the summer of 1999, "The odds of correctly pinpointing the future returns, deviations, and correlations for several asset classes are well below those of winning $20 million from Ed McMahon. Which means that, by definition, the efficient frontier is anything but."

THINGS CHANGE

Market veterans are fond of saying, "The four most dangerous words in investing are *this time it's different.*" What they are trying to say is that what often looks like change is merely a new gloss on an old pattern, and that to conclude that we are significantly deviating from the expected norm could prove costly. A cliché, to be sure. But like many clichés, it does contain a germ of truth. As it may apply to human nature, the cliché may well represent some wisdom. Our emotions, our thought patterns, our entire range of actions and motivations are the result of tens of thousands of years of evolution. They are "hardwired," so to speak, into our nervous system and remain relevant predictors of behavior, regardless of current fad or fashion. Fear, euphoria, greed, and panic are just some of the ways these biological "constants" manifest themselves in the financial markets.

It is important, however, to separate the "creation that is man" from "man's creation." Two very different concepts; we confuse the two at our own peril. The structure and the nature of the world that we build around us are *always changing*.

The most extreme example of this concept occurred when the first atomic bombs were dropped in 1945. After this event, every thoughtful person knew, immediately and intuitively, that this time it was different. The world had changed, irrevocably. The weapons of war that a great power would now have at its disposal had forever changed the nature of conflict. The stakes had been raised to a level previously only contemplated in apocalyptic fiction. Those on the real life playing field needed to understand and act on this realization.

At the same time, wise leaders also knew that *human nature* had not suddenly changed just because the technology to split the atom had been perfected. The same fears, suspicions, hopes, animosities and aspirations that drove leaders before Hiroshima were still operative. We needed to understand and be aware of this as well.

Investors who perform historical asset class correlation studies fall into the trap of not differentiating between the unchanging patterns of human *nature* and the constantly changing patterns and relationships among the *structures* humans create. Thus, the response to change from the informed asset allocator is likely to be simple denial. Practitioners are hesitant to discard decades of correlation data on the contention (always unproven, since only time can "prove" change) that "things are different now." But reality won't just go away. When it intrudes on their carefully constructed models, however, they unfortunately chide the messenger for thinking that things could really be different this time. They might just as well hang a sign on their doors saying, "Don't confuse me with the facts. My mind is made up."

WHEN THINGS CHANGED

By being resistant to change before years of confirming data have accumulated, asset allocators often incur monumental risks. A classic example is the historic change that occurred in the yield relationship between stocks and bonds in the late 1950s. Until that time, stocks had historically yielded more than bonds. This seemed to be simple common sense: stocks, after all, carried more risk. Investors ought to be rewarded for assuming that risk by receiving a higher dividend. There had been periods before when stocks had appreciated so sharply that their yield fell below that of bonds. Inevitably, that had signaled an overvalued market that was due for—and ultimately experienced—a sharp decline.

So here we are in the late 1950s. An extended bull run in stocks has pulled the yield on equities once again below that of bonds. "Aha!" say the asset allocators, "Time to sell stocks. They are overpriced and due for a correction." Unfortunately for them, the correction never did come. (At least not for a long, long time, and not in the way they expected.) Things had changed and this time it really was different. The relationship between stocks and bonds had been transformed in the crucible of the post–World War II economy and would never again revert to its former dynamic. Those who insisted on adhering to the old norms stayed away from the "overvalued" stock market and missed the huge bull market of the 1960s.

More recently, strategists married to unchanging historic relationships bemoaned the decline in yield on the S&P 500. A decade ago, they were in full "Chicken Little" mode about how the market's yield had fallen below 3.5%, historically an extreme danger signal. (This, of course, was 7000 Dow points ago.) By these guys' lights, a 50% decline in the Dow would still leave us slightly overvalued. Yet most rational observers doubt that we'll ever see stock yields get back to the levels seen in the past. Things have changed. This time it *is* different.

Even something as basic as the correlation between stocks and bonds has changed radically over the past 75 years. According to Jeremy Siegel in *Stocks for the Long Run*, the correlation coefficient between annual stock and bond returns from 1926–1969 was -0.02. This means that not only didn't stocks and bonds move in similar directions, they actually moved in slightly opposite directions most of the time. (A correlation coefficient of +1 means the two assets being compared moved in exactly the same way; a correlation coefficient of -1 means the two assets being compared moved in exactly the opposite direction. Coefficients between -1 and +1 reflect the range of variations of how assets move relative to each other.) Younger investors who have grown up in a world where the health of the bond and stock markets have been generally linked might find this slight negative correlation unusual.

Yet the same relationship measured from 1970–1989 showed a correlation coefficient of .39. Bonds, while not moving in lockstep with stocks, were clearly moving much more similarly than they had done over the previous 50 years. From 1990–1997, the number had increased to .62, showing an even greater similarity of movements. Clearly, bonds in the 1990s were not hedging stocks nearly as effectively as they had done for preceding generations. This was a natural reflection of the fact that inflation, rather than depression, was the major risk for the markets in modern times. Thus we find ourselves in the rather unusual circumstance of having both stocks and bonds subject to much the same macro risks. It wasn't always this way.

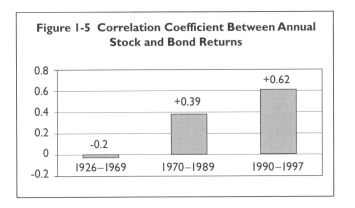

Figure 1-5 Correlation Coefficient Between Annual Stock and Bond Returns

Source: *Stocks for the Long Run 2nd Ed.*, Jeremy Siegel, McGraw Hill, N.Y., 1998. Reproduced with permission of The McGraw-Hill Companies

REGRESSION TO THE MEAN

Because their worldview is so statistically based, investors enamored of diversification and asset allocation strategies often base decisions on *regression (or reversion) to the mean* strategies. Regression to the mean says that things won't move too far for too long. Eventually, everything adjusts to a long-term statistical average or norm. When someone says something like "The trees don't grow to the sky," they're illustrating this concept. There is nothing wrong with this. The concept of regression to the mean not only has validity in numerous circumstances, but has been the source of many a famous investor's coups. Think about the cliché of "buy low, sell high." The thought behind it is that what goes up will likely come down, and what has come down will likely go up, as prices regress to the mean.

We must, at the same time, remember that regression to the mean, as a tool for forecasting the future, can be a dangerous strategy. Sometimes the regression happens much more slowly than expected; sometime the mean itself (as we just saw in the examples of stock/bond yield relationships and the dividend level of the S&P) is in the process of changing.

Tactical asset allocation: the slippery slope

Even if we could, just for the sake of discussion, accept the fact that historic relationships and correlations are accurate, relevant and useful tools, we are still faced with the basic, faulty imperative dictated by modern asset allocation: *Reduction of risk is equated with reduction of volatility.*

This leads to the worst of all possible strategies: *tactical asset allocation.* The really bad news is that's exactly the toxic advice you're fed every day by the media.

Make no mistake about it; tactical asset allocation is to investors what Kryptonite is to Superman. So what is it? Why is it so dangerous? And why is it so hard to avoid?

Strategic and tactical asset allocation

There are two broad asset allocation frameworks, *strategic* asset allocation and *tactical* asset allocation. Strategic asset allocation refers to the long-term approach you take so that your portfolio will reflect your objectives, your risk tolerances, and your long-term goals. An example of a strategic asset allocation would be a broad division of your portfolio into, say 60% stocks and 40% bonds. Regardless of how the market is performing over any short to intermediate period, you would be very unlikely to change this mix. Adjustment would be made only if your personal circumstances changed to a significant degree.

Tactical asset allocation is a framework which requires you to "tweak" your allocation to either increase your potential return or decrease your risk. Some examples of tactical asset allocation moves: shifting dollars from U.S. funds to international funds; reducing your small-cap exposure and buying large-cap funds; raising cash to deal with potential market risks.

What I have found so ironic is that almost every experienced professional in the fund industry will deride tactical asset allocation, yet it is almost universally practiced—even by many of those folks who scoff at its efficacy! Think about the moves you've made with your portfolio over the past several years. Chances are you've engaged in tactical asset allocation at one time or another. Tactical asset allocation is the mother's milk of the financial world. Without it, the investment media would have little or nothing to report on a regular basis. Every financial publication regularly runs articles that urgently relate, "Ten Moves You Should Make Now!" or "Top Fund Picks For 1995" or 1996, or 1997, or 1998 and so on and so on....

So commonplace is this attitude that we have even lost sight of the absurdity of publishing regular lists of "The Best Funds." As a consumer I wonder, when I read this year's list of best funds, what I'm supposed to do with the *different* list of best funds I bought last year? Is it still the best? If not, why not, and what should I do?

Tactical asset allocation is so pervasive that it is not even labeled as such when it's printed in mass-market publications. A remarkable example of unlabeled tactical asset allocation was seen in one of *Money* magazine's regular "essential guides" to the best funds. In a sidebar titled, "Building the Perfect Portfolio," an allocation that purports to be a "fine-tuning" of a more basic approach looks like this:

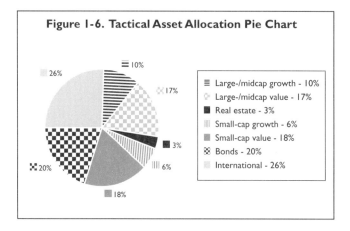

Figure 1-6. Tactical Asset Allocation Pie Chart

≡ Large-/midcap growth - 10%
✧ Large-/midcap value - 17%
■ Real estate - 3%
▨ Small-cap growth - 6%
▩ Small-cap value - 18%
▨ Bonds - 20%
▨ International - 26%

Nowhere does *Money* state that this is a "radical" approach. It is offered as a professionally derived, prudent mix. Yet radical it is. Some 24% of the portfolio is allocated to small-cap stocks, either growth or value, out of a total of 54% that is allocated to the U.S. stock market. No doubt this is at least partly due to the advisor's view that small caps represent greater value at this point in time over large caps (a tactical decision). Sounds reasonable until you calculate that 24% represents 44% of the dollars this advisor allocated to the U.S. market. Since small caps (stocks with market caps of $1.1 billion or less) represent only about 8% of U.S. market capitalization, this portfolio is recommending a gross overweighting in small caps—*more than five times the market weight!* Viewed from this perspective, this "fine-tuned" mix is an enormously risky tactical move. If small caps continue to underperform, this portfolio will have no chance of achieving decent returns. In any case, over the long term, few professionals would recommend a 44% allocation to small caps. *At some point, this portfolio will be subject to another decision—when to cut back on small caps.*

We could fill an entire book with similar examples, but anyone who listens to CNBC or reads major financial publications on a daily basis has been exposed to this often enough.

DON'T JUST STAND THERE, DO SOMETHING!

Tactical asset allocation is ultimately disastrous because it perverts the natural order of things. It shifts the focus of a long-term portfolio to the short term, thus creating a contradiction of purpose that can't help but negatively impact results. We regularly hear advice that tells us to eliminate or reduce holdings in a sector that holds great long-term growth prospects because of perceived (or even real!) overvaluation or the risk of a short-term correction. When we follow this advice, we make the mistake of taking our eye off the long-term profit potential of a position in favor of trying to maximize short-term market moves. That may be fine for traders, but it should be obvious that it runs counter to what we, as long-term investors, should be doing. If you are an investor with a 10–20 year time horizon, shifting assets based on how you think tech stocks, for example, may perform over the next 6–12 months is, frankly, schizophrenic. And seldom right. Yet the media regularly comes up with new strategies of what to buy, sell, add, cut

back on, etc. in order to help you survive "_____"
(fill in the crisis du jour).

Smart Money, in its November 1998 issue (which hit the
stands around mid-October) was only one of many that over-
reacted to the short-term craziness of the summer/fall decline.
They wrote: *"Here's what we suggest: A weak economy allocation
makes the most sense right now. Even though the U.S. economy may
escape recession next year, as long as global deflation and falling
interest rates continue, the extra bond allocation will result in higher returns."*

We now know, even as these words were being printed, that
great earnings were being reported and the U.S. economy continued to surge ahead. In fact, the biggest risk over the past year
has been to bonds, not stocks. In this case, as in so many others, we see in hindsight that the crisis was nothing more than
an inconsequential blip on the long-term pattern of the market. And the move turned out to be counterproductive.

Sure, it's easy to make fun from a distance. I assure you that
my pontifications over the years have also contained gems right
up there with *Smart Money's.* (I still shudder when I remember
a report I sent to my clients in the fall of 1996 that declared the
U.S. market to be overvalued and poised to "regress to the
mean." I was especially negative on the S&P. That, of course,
was several thousand Dow points ago! Brother, what a bad call
that was.)

So why do otherwise intelligent people make the same mistakes over and over? I think this tendency to overreact in the
short term is a direct consequence of working within the tactical asset allocation model. There is a natural human tendency
to use tools that are made available to us. If you begin with the
premise that there are many different asset classes to choose

from, and then assume that there is a time and a place when one will help to counterbalance the other, should we be surprised that investors would avail themselves of the opportunities this presents?

On the other hand, what if you assumed that there were not multiple asset classes to choose from? What if you didn't believe that one asset class would effectively balance out another? Wouldn't there be less temptation to make short-term adjustments? One can remain realistic about short-term market valuations without feeling that action is always required. Legendary investor Warren Buffet will, from time to time, observe that the market is overvalued; that doesn't mean that he then proceeds to sell his Coca-Cola stock. Were you to make such a suggestion to him, he might jokingly reply, "Just which words in the phrase 'long-term investor' don't you understand?"

The constant drumbeat of news, both positive and negative, along with the regular lists of "things to do," inevitably take their toll. Rare is the investor, civilian or professional, who can long withstand the modern media onslaught. Yet, because the media by its very nature is reporting what has *previously* happened, investors often find themselves reacting to events that have already passed them by. *Almost inevitably, the tendency thus becomes to buy after a run up has already happened and sell after a decline has already occurred.* More money becomes invested at asset class peaks; less money is left in the till at asset class lows. The sad result is that the return of the average shareholder in an asset class is likely to be considerably less than the return of the asset class itself over the same period.

Figures 1–7, 1–8, and 1–9 graphically show this dysfunctional cash flow/return dynamic with small caps, emerging markets, and real estate investments. As you can see, the big chunk of

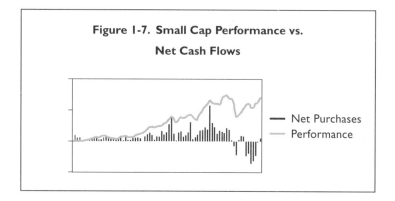

Figure 1-7. Small Cap Performance vs.
Net Cash Flows

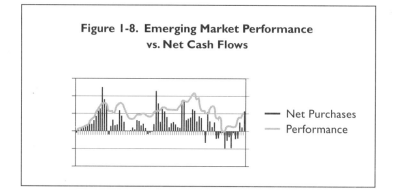

Figure 1-8. Emerging Market Performance
vs. Net Cash Flows

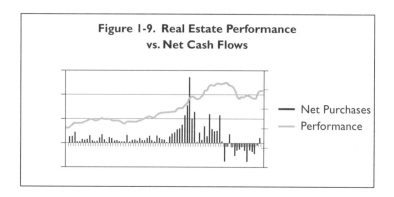

Figure 1-9. Real Estate Performance
vs. Net Cash Flows

investor dollars flow in after extended periods of good performance and flow out after things have gotten bad. Is this any way to run a railroad?

Every mutual fund organization knows this to be true. They all have horror stories about investor cash flows and some have done detailed studies that show how much return investors have sacrificed by moving dollars around. The funds, though, are by no means blameless in this. It has long been observed that mutual fund companies, since they usually tend to sell performance, will tout a specific fund only after it has had a significant run-up. They thus help create the dynamic by which dollars flow into specific funds at interim tops. The tragedy is that by the time long-term investors realize how much tactical asset allocation has cost them, it is too late to do anything. Great potential wealth has already been squandered in pursuit of a chimerical goal.

The first step on the road back to sanity is to commit to a buy and hold strategy. Not much of a revelation, I'll admit. Many others have said the same thing many times before. What's different in our analysis, however, is our exploration of what you hold. *A buy and hold strategy won't be of much help if what you're holding is garbage.* If anything, it will only magnify your mistakes. In Part Two of this book we'll give you specific advice on how to solve this dilemma. For now, though, let's look at some of the more egregious examples of hazardous allocations resulting from conventional approaches to diversification.

CHAPTER TWO

THE SMALL CAP HOAX

*"The problem ain't what we don't know
but what we do know that ain't true."*
Will Rogers

IT'S NEARLY IMPOSSIBLE to read about mutual funds without coming across the ubiquitous statement that small-cap stocks have, over time, outperformed their large-cap cousins. This bit of dogma has been so universally accepted that folks are regularly told to place anywhere from 15–35% of their portfolio in small-cap stock funds.

Small-cap superiority seems to be an easy premise to accept. It intuitively "feels" right that a company that is starting small would, if successful, grow at a greater percentage rate than a larger, more mature company. If we link risk and reward, given the obviously greater risk inherent in small company stocks, why shouldn't they do better than large company stocks?

Of course, we all know that has not been the case in recent years. A remarkable run of underperformance on the part of small caps has been one of the things that has caused asset allocators so much grief lately. We wondered: Have we missed something? Has the large cap/small cap dynamic changed? Were our, and the industry's, original assumptions correct in the first place?

Clearly, we needed to step back and re-acquaint ourselves with what the story was.

In the late 1970s, a graduate student named Rolf Banz did the original research that led to the "discovery" of small-cap superiority. He went back to 1926 and tracked the returns of both large and small stocks over time. He divided all the stocks listed on the New York Stock Exchange into ten groupings by size (deciles). He labeled the top two deciles "large caps" and the bottom two deciles, "small caps." He found that, even after allowing for risk (volatility), the smallest two deciles far outstripped the performance of the largest two deciles. As the chart below shows, there seems to be a clear correlation between size and return.

Figure 2-1. Long-Term Returns of New York Stock Exchange Stocks Ranked by Size			
Size Decile	**Compound Annual Return 1926-1996**	**Largest Firm in Decile as of Sept. 1996**	**Largest Firm in Decile as of June 1999***
Largest	9.84%	$150.26B	$369.72B
2	11.06%	$6.95B	$10.84B
3	11.49%	$3.24B	$4.33B
4	11.63%	$1.89B	$2.30B
5	12.16%	$1.15B	$1.37B
6	11.82%	$755M	$891M
7	11.88%	$521M	$606M
8	12.15%	$336M	$393M
9	12.25%	$197M	$230M
Smallest	13.83%	$94M	$105M

Source: Jeremy J. Siegel, *Stocks for the Long Run, 2nd Edition* (New York: McGraw-Hill, 1998), page 93.

*Source: Dimensional Fund Advisors.

This data appears to be strong and irrefutable, until you begin to look beneath the numbers. We found that these numbers were based on methodologies and inferences that are, to put it bluntly, bogus. Respected and successful money manager David Dreman has performed remarkable research in this area. In his most recent book[1], Dreman gives the most detailed and perceptive analysis of historical small-cap statistics that you'll ever find. The only thing more astonishing than what he uncovered is that the investment industry has ignored his explosive evidence.

SMALL-CAP PERFORMANCE IN CONTEXT

A more detailed breakdown of Banz's performance numbers shows that the first period of tremendous outperformance by "small" companies was 1931–1935. This struck us as a bit odd; anyone familiar with the economic history of the Depression years knows that those times were particularly tough on the fortunes of small companies. Just remaining in business was a questionable proposition. How is it that small company stocks could do so much better than their equally troubled, but more financially secure, larger brethren?

Dreman has written that these performance numbers were not really those of true small-cap stocks! By 1931, many blue chips had been devastated by the onset of the Great Depression. Their stock prices had plummeted to a fraction of their former value. They now fell into the "small cap" deciles. The true small caps of the day were not to be found on the NYSE, even in the bottom two deciles.

---

1 Reprinted with the permission of Simon and Schuster from *Contrarian Investment Strategies* by David Dreman, Copyright " © 1998 by David Dreman. pp. 317–323.

How these smallest stocks were grouped and tracked was an often-overlooked element of the study. The stocks in the smallest two deciles were tracked for *five-year periods*. Even if a stock in this group grew in the first year or two so that it would no longer be in the bottom two deciles, *it still remained in the measured group*. When the "busted" large caps that found themselves at the bottom of the pack in 1931 bounced back over the following years, they were counted as small caps that had performed tremendously. Thus, this famous study showed that in the 1931–1935 period small stocks outperformed large stocks by an outlandishly large 101% to 17% margin. I think it would be generous to call this kind of measurement misleading, to say the least.

Figure 2-2. "Small-Cap" Returns, 1931-1935	
1931	-49.75%
1932	-5.39%
1933	142.87%
1934	24.22%
1935	40.19%

Soon thereafter, we are confronted with another statistical aberration that is understandable only when viewed within the context of the times. During the 1941–1945 period, "small caps" gained over 650% while the largest companies had to settle for about 140%. This is an astonishing margin for such a short period, but one that is easily explainable. What happened? World War II.

Contrary to popular myth, the New Deal did not pull the U.S. out of the Depression. At the onset of the war, economic activity was still extremely sluggish and unemployment high. FDR had admittedly managed to stave off a complete collapse of the American system, and had given Americans hope that things would eventually get better, but the bottom line was that the economy still seemed to be stuck in first gear.

The war changed all that. Overnight, the "arsenal of democracy" went to work—overtime. Again, companies that were formerly much larger were limping along in the bottom two deciles at the time. Come the war, their fortunes revived and boom! Goodbye bottom-decile status. But remember, in one of the study's major flaws, they were kept in the small-cap category for five years.

Figure 2-3. Small-Cap Returns, 1941-1945

1941	-9.00%
1942	44.51%
1943	88.37%
1944	53.72%
1945	73.61%

So for the first twenty years of the study, a twenty-year period that ostensibly showed tremendous small-cap outperformance, what we were really seeing was the rebounding of busted large caps. We were not seeing merely the dynamic growth of newer, small enterprises.

REAL-LIFE TRADING
IS NOT DONE IN IVORY TOWERS

The most astonishing aspect of the market and small caps during this period was the reality of trading. Here is where the numbers quoted in the study become not just questionable, but actually absurd.

As Dreman revealed, the market in these smaller stocks was remarkably illiquid during this period. The average volume of these bottom-two-decile stocks during the 1931–1935 period was *240 shares per day.* And that number is only as high as it is due to a few more heavily traded issues. The median volume was *100 shares a day. Over half of the stocks did not even trade on a given day!*

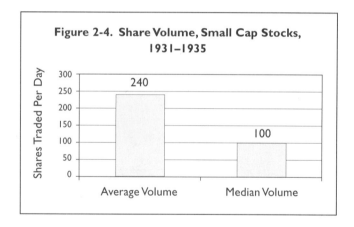

Figure 2-4. Share Volume, Small Cap Stocks, 1931–1935

As you can imagine, spreads were enormous. The difference between the bid and the ask price averaged some 45%. (The spread is the difference between the ask price—what you pay when you buy—and the bid price—what you get when you sell. For instance, a stock might be quoted at $10 asked and $9.75 bid. The spread in this case is 25 cents. If the spread were 45%, you would have to pay $10 for the stock but only get $5.50 if you turned around and immediately sold. Obviously, with spreads that large, it is very, very difficult to make any money.) Banz's study, however, did not realistically take this into account, nor did it factor in commissions.

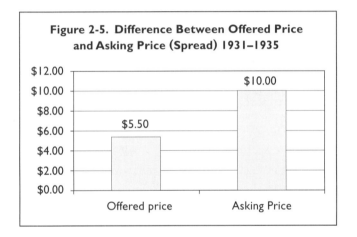

By the 1941–45 period, things had loosened up, but only by comparison. Trading volume on these smaller issues had "swelled" to almost 500 shares per day. Spreads were a still-large 17%. (We should note that lower volume and increased spreads also affected larger stocks, but not nearly to the extent as in the smallest two deciles.)

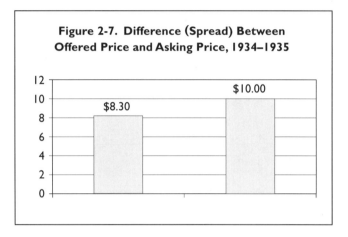

Figure 2-7. Difference (Spread) Between
Offered Price and Asking Price, 1934–1935

As practical investors, we were left scratching our heads. The information in Banz's study was so divorced from the actuality of real market execution as to be rendered totally useless. Even if you could take a time machine back to 1931 in hopes of benefiting from what this research revealed, you still couldn't reap much benefit. The market reality was that much of your profits would be eroded due to the costs of illiquidity and commissions. As Dreman noted, these errors "...stemmed from contemporary financial researchers' near obsession with statistical tests, applied all too often with little understanding of the underlying data or market mechanisms."

Remarkably, even "front loading" the data with incredible, if unreplicatable, performance, small caps still barely beat large caps by 1975. (And, if you honestly counted trading costs, actually lagged!) So we had a fifty-year period of higher risk but no higher returns. So far, the accurate historic record is not looking good for small caps.

In the modern era, the glory years for small caps were 1975–1983, when the bottom two deciles averaged over 35% per year, smoking the almost 16% annual returns for the large caps. While the Depression is history book stuff for most of us, this, now, was current history. This was real.

Figure 2-3. Small-Cap Returns, 1975-1983	
1975	52.82%
1976	57.38%
1977	25.38%
1978	23.46%
1979	43.46%
1980	39.88%
1981	13.88%
1982	28.01%
1983	39.67%

But when we thought about that period (again that dreaded context!) we wondered whether it made for a stronger—or weaker—small-cap argument today.

In addition to bad hair, bad clothes, and bad music, the 1975–83 period had bad corporate culture. Large U.S. companies, riding a quarter century post-war boom in which they had little or no serious competition, had grown fat, lazy, sloppy, and arrogant. They were setting themselves up for the classic fall. Into this environment came the lean and hungry Japanese and Germans with business models far more efficient and flexible. They found a large-cap America weakened by the effects of massive increases in energy prices. Recall that back then, much more so than now, blue-chip America was dominated by old "industrial era" companies, wasteful heavy manufacturing concerns that were much more energy dependent. No question about it, this was a much more benign environment for smaller, more nimble and creative companies.

But even though this is of relatively recent memory, how relevant is the dynamic it describes to our world today? The large caps of today are more likely to be aggressive, efficient information-based companies like Microsoft, Intel, Merck and GE. While we can debate whether inflation might tick up a bit as we move ahead, no reasonable observer would suggest one should plan for a renewed bout of commodity-induced double digit inflation. And even if we somehow did see a resurgence of inflation, would the effect on the information-based large caps of the 1990s be the same as it was on the industrial large caps of the 1970s? In short, the very things that held back large caps in the 1975–83 period are simply nonfactors today.

We concluded two things after looking more closely at the historic numbers and underlying environments. First, much of the pure data—particularly that of the early years—is useless from a practical standpoint. It is far too disconnected from the reality of actual trading activity to be predictive of anything. Second, the more recent small-cap outperformance occurred during a period that while seemingly of our own era, is so dissimilar to our current dynamic that one hesitates to project anything from it.

Do we thus conclude that small caps will *never* outperform large caps? Of course not. It's a pretty safe bet that there will be some periods when the best gains are to be found in smaller companies. *We can conclude, and say with certainty, that the commonly accepted wisdom about small-cap outperformance is false, and that the "groundbreaking" research that helped to create this myth is an embarrassment to the entire industry.*

AND FURTHERMORE...

Let's just say, for the sake of discussion, that we could accept the notion, as suggested by research, that small caps outperform large caps over time. We're still left with the problematic question: What do we mean by small cap? The Banz study used as a small-cap proxy the lowest two deciles on the N.Y. Stock Exchange. Today, that would mean a universe of stocks with a median market cap of under $150 million. Yet the median market cap of funds in the Morningstar small cap categories is about $900 million. That size market cap would be more reflective of companies in the fifth decile of the NYSE, not the bottom two deciles. As figure 2.1 (page 48) shows, the level of outperformance of those deciles is much lower.

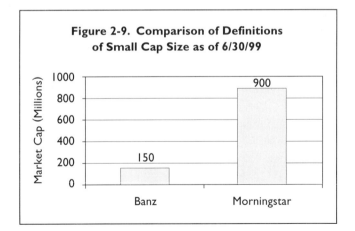

Figure 2-9. Comparison of Definitions of Small Cap Size as of 6/30/99

There is one fund, however, that has scrupulously adhered to selection only of stocks that fall within the bottom two deciles. The fund is the DFA 9/10 Fund. DFA (Dimensional Fund Advisors) was the first mutual fund organization to aggressively market its product using the historical studies that "proved" the superiority of small-cap stocks. The firm prominently highlights its connection to the leading academics that helped to create and promote the small-cap story. The DFA 9/10 Fund has, since its inception in 1982, returned 13.72% annualized through 6/30/99. The S&P 500 has returned almost 18.4% annualized over the same period. This means that an investment of $10,000 in the DFA 9/10 Fund at inception in 1982 would have been worth $94,873 on June 30, 1999 whereas an investment of $10,000 in the S&P 500 would have been worth $197,802; more than double! The DFA 9/10 Fund shareholders continue to patiently await the much-heralded "small-cap advantage."

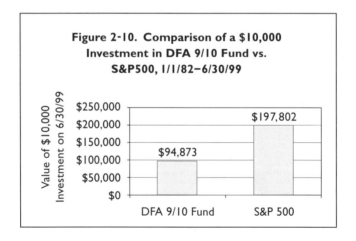

Figure 2-10. Comparison of a $10,000 Investment in DFA 9/10 Fund vs. S&P500, 1/1/82–6/30/99

CHAPTER THREE

INTERNATIONAL INVESTING: HOW TO DISAPPOINT YOURSELF IN TWELVE LANGUAGES

"It's hard enough to understand the peculiarities and complexities of the culture in which you've been raised, much less a variety of others."

Warren Buffet

CONVENTIONAL WISDOM tells us that diversifying internationally is smart for two reasons. First, there is the belief that international markets are generally not highly correlated with the U.S. market and do not always move in the same direction at the same time as we do here. Because they often times "zig" when we "zag," it is believed that international investments can help to reduce the volatility of a portfolio. The conventional wisdom also tells us international investments offer the opportunity for significant upside gain. After all, the reasoning goes, some two-thirds of the world's companies are in countries outside of the U.S. There must be tremendous opportunities in that large universe of companies. Why would we want to exclude them from our portfolio? It's a compelling argument, one that I myself believed and used many times over the years.

Unfortunately, reality does not support the dogma.

CORRELATION: MYTH AND REALITY

Do international markets really exhibit low correlation to the U.S. market? Some argue that all markets around the globe are becoming increasingly correlated, and that the benefits of international diversification—from a correlation standpoint—no longer exist. Others maintain that the data shows that foreign markets are, indeed, still largely noncorrelated with the U.S. Our work tells us that, amazingly, both are true.

As investors in the U.S., with the bulk of our portfolios invested in U.S. funds, we would naturally look to our foreign diversification to help us during difficult periods here in the U.S. Unfortunately, that hasn't happened very often.

Between 1970 and 1998, there have been five years in which the S&P 500 had a negative return. The average loss of those five negative years was 11.3%. In only *one* of those five years did the EAFE go up when the S&P fell. (EAFE is Morgan Stanley's index of Europe, Australia, and the Far East, an industry-accepted benchmark for international investment comparisons.) The average of the five years in question for the EAFE was a *negative 11.5%*.

Figure 3-1. S&P 500 Negative Years vs. EAFE

YEAR	S&P 500	EAFE
1990	-3.17%	-24.71%
1981	-4.91%	-4.85%
1977	-7.18%	14.61%
1974	-26.47%	-25.60%
1973	-14.66%	-16.82%
Avg.	-11.28%	-11.47%

Source: Morgan Stanley Capital International, Inc.

From where we sit, the long-term record seems pretty clear: There is absolutely no evidence to suggest that you can count on international diversification to act as a cushion during declining markets here in the U.S.

(A fascinating side note: While it doesn't appear that foreign markets hedge the U.S. very well, U.S. markets may be a good hedge against declines overseas. Again, going back to 1970, there have been eight years when the EAFE declined. The average decline was 13.1%. The average return for the S&P during those eight years was a *positive 0.97%!* So yes, overseas diversification may help you cushion the downside—if you live and invest in Frankfurt!)

Figure 3-2. EAFE Negative Years vs. S&P 500		
YEAR	S&P 500	EAFE
1992	7.67%	-13.89%
1990	-3.17%	-24.71%
1982	21.41%	-4.63%
1981	-4.91%	-4.85%
1976	23.84%	-0.36%
1974	-26.47%	-25.60%
1973	-14.66%	-16.82%
1970	4.01%	-14.13%
Ave.	+.97%	-13.10%

Source: Morgan Stanley Capital International, Inc.

What is particularly compelling about these numbers is that the last year covered was 1994. (There have been no negative years in the U.S. since then.) Thus, the data *does not* include the remarkable relative performance of the U.S. market in the 1995–1998 period, making the comparisons about as fair to the internationalists as they could possibly be.

The more we look into the numbers, the clearer it becomes that the whole correlation story as it applies to foreign investments is, astonishingly, *opposite* from what we've been taught to expect. During times of great volatility, during the bear markets that we all dread, foreign stocks and U.S. stocks move in remarkable lockstep.

The 1973–1974 bear market, the 1987 crash, and the 1998 global financial crisis all wreaked havoc on investors in both domestic and foreign markets. Investors were little better off for their foreign diversification. In fact, one could make a case that the opposite was just as likely to be the case—that one's *foreign* holdings could actually be a drag on performance.

Figure 3.3 S&P 500 vs. Foreign and Emerging Market Funds

Period	S&P 500	Avg. Foreign Fund	Avg. Emerging Market Fund
1/73–9/74	-48.4%	-39.2%*	na
9/87–11/87	-30.0%	-22.5%	-32.0%
8/98–9/98	-8.5%	-17.3%	-26.0%

*EAFE used for '73–'74 period due to the lack of a substantive number of foreign funds in that period.

Ironically, foreign markets show the greatest degree of non-correlation during relatively calm or positive periods here in the

U.S. So those who claim that foreign markets have not become more correlated with the U.S. in recent years are factually correct, but not for the reason they suppose. Foreign markets have, indeed, not moved similar to the U.S. *They've done much worse!* The most obvious example is Japan. While U.S. stocks have soared over the past decade, Japanese stocks saw their values cut in half. Diversify into the Japanese market and, yes, you would have reduced your portfolio's volatility. Problem is, it would have been upward volatility that would have been sacrificed as Japanese losses eroded your domestic gains. I'm not sure that was quite the "smoothing out of the ride" that financial planners like to refer to when they talk about diversification and noncorrelation.

Our conclusion can only be that the conventional wisdom regarding foreign market correlation has more than a few holes in it. While the historic record does show instances where an investment overseas would have added stability in your portfolio due to noncorrelation, those instances have, unfortunately, been brief and infrequent. More often than not, international diversification leads to motion sickness and indigestion, not stability and peace of mind.

IS THE UPSIDE THERE?

What about the special potential for gain that is always included in the benefits of foreign diversification? Correlations aside, if one can make more money overseas than here in the U.S., shouldn't that be reason enough to include foreign funds in a growth portfolio? Certainly any reasonable person would have to say yes. But once again, the assumption that is all too easily made—that foreign investments have the ability to perform equal to or better than U.S. stocks—is difficult to prove in real life.

What the advocates of foreign diversification fail to fully disclose is that investments in foreign markets exhibit a degree of downside volatility a good deal greater on a yearly basis than those in the U.S. Since 1970, the S&P 500 has suffered a double-digit annual loss twice. Over the same period, the EAFE has plunged into the double digits five times. Has that added volatility been rewarded in enhanced return? Absolutely not. From 1970 through 1998, the S&P 500 compounded at 13.5%. Over that same period, the EAFE generated a mere 9.5% annual return. (If you're wondering why we picked the period beginning in 1970, that simply was the furthest back we could go and still get data that was reliable.)

The results generated by mutual funds in the international arena give little comfort to those who promote the upside potential of foreign markets. The past fifteen years are very illuminating. During this period, each of the asset classes we are discussing has had its "time in the sun," so to speak. The mid '80s were a great time for broad international funds. The late '80s to early '90s saw remarkable returns in emerging markets. The mid to late '90s were clearly the time for the U.S. markets to shine. So each asset class had "its shot." When all was said and done, over the fifteen years, the S&P 500 compounded at 17.9% while the average foreign fund gained just 13.0% annually.

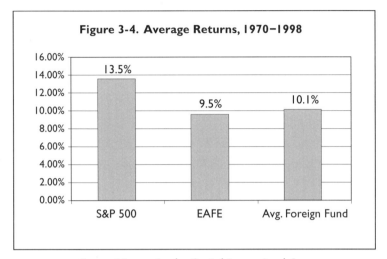

Source: Morgan Stanley Capital International, Inc.

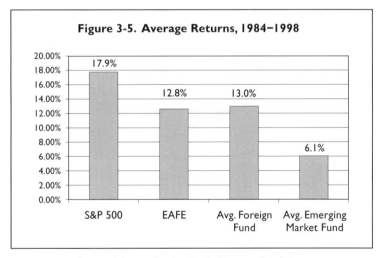

Source: Morgan Stanley Capital International, Inc.

Overall, foreign investments have not only underperformed, they have exposed you to more periods of negative annual performance.

THE EMERGING MARKETS SCAM

Aggressive growth investors are often counseled to put a portion of their money in emerging markets funds. Even if they choose not to do so and stick to regular international funds, they still end up with a big chunk of their foreign holdings in emerging markets. This, theoretically, is where the really big payoffs are supposed to be. And certainly this has been the case for short periods. From 12/1/92 through 1/31/94, a period of just 14 months, the average emerging markets fund gained 79.2%. Unfortunately, they then proceeded to slip into a performance coma for the next three years. From 2/1/94 through 1/31/97 the total return in this category was a miniscule 1.1%. But that, apparently, was just the lull before the storm. From 2/1/97 through 12/31/98, the average emerging market fund suffered a devastating 34.5% loss. The net result is that the long-term share-holder in the average emerging market fund spent the last six years on a roller coaster only to see an annualized return of 2.7%. High risk, low returns. What's wrong with this picture?

Even when we look longer term for buy-and-hold investors, this volatility does not seem to have been rewarded. One dollar invested in 1970 in the fast growing Pacific Rim markets (not including Japan) grew to $5.12 by the end of 1998. By contrast, one dollar invested in the S&P in 1970 grew to $17.58 by the end of 1998. I think this is extremely significant. Over the past thirty years, the economies of the "tigers" of East Asia have seen explosive growth. Starting from a virtual standstill in 1970, they are now vital economic powerhouses. If, in that period of astonishing up-from-nowhere growth, their markets could not return but one-third of the U.S., when will the payoff ever come?

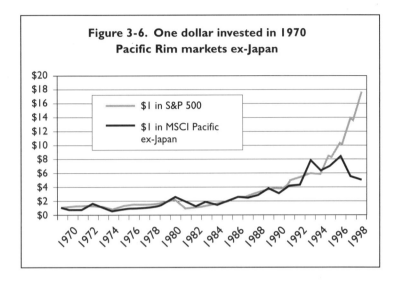

Figure 3-6. One dollar invested in 1970
Pacific Rim markets ex-Japan

Even under ideal circumstances, investing for superior long-term returns is a difficult challenge. Investing in the emerging markets is like trying to play a game with no rulebook and no referee. The remarkable lack of regulatory oversight, the astonishing corruption at even the highest level, the frightening lack of clear and honest disclosure are too often soft-pedaled by those who make these investments. Given the existence of these very real risks, and given that they manifest themselves in different ways and different times as one looks at Russia, Korea, South America, et al., the amazing part is that anyone sane thinks any money manager can truly get his arms around the situation. Or that average investors should even consider these vehicles. Imagine the U.S. market without the SEC. Imagine a political environment where President Clinton, or close aides, scheme behind the scenes with Bill Gates to enrich themselves secretly. Imagine Cabinet secretaries taking payoffs from the latest hot Internet company to fudge some regulatory rule. This unimaginable environment is exactly what the investor in emerging markets must confront daily. Insane.

Emerging market investors (and here I'm including financial planners, investment advisors, journalists and regular consumers) have fallen hook, line and sinker for the "myth of the emerging markets guru." It seems every fund company markets its special management team that has an intimate and in-depth knowledge of these exotic markets. They can, the story goes, help guide us through the complex ins and outs of this most rewarding investment class. Baloney. The facts point to these "experts" as nothing more than individuals who were adept at piloting the boat during a rising tide. When we as investors really needed their expertise, they were 100% AWOL. Did any of these geniuses see the Asian currency crisis coming in 1997? How many of them were caught flatfooted by the Russian default and ensuing crisis in 1998? One of the dirty little secrets of the fund world is that these managers are getting paid huge fees (the average management fee in an emerging market fund is 2.13%) for doing little more than holding on tight to the roller coaster.

THE CURRENCY WILD CARD

The value of the U.S. dollar relative to foreign currencies has a significant impact on returns that an investor will likely see in an international fund. This is a complex area, but the simplified bottom line is that when the U.S. dollar is weak relative to overseas currencies, returns on foreign investments will be enhanced. When the U.S. dollar is strong, foreign returns will most likely be diminished. Over extended periods these ups and downs tend to even themselves out and we can see what the pure economic-driven return has been. Short term, however, currency fluctuations can skew returns enormously.

Why is this important to know? It helps us to put into context shorter-term data. For example, many international investing proponents will point to the remarkable performance of foreign investments relative to the U.S. during the period of about 1985 until 1994 as proof of the value of having some of your portfolio overseas.

Figure 3-7. S&P 500 vs. Foreign Fund Returns, 1985–1993		
Year	S&P 500	Average Foreign Fund
1993	9.99%	36.74%
1992	7.67%	-4.54%
1991	30.55%	13.07%
1990	-3.17%	-10.90%
1989	31.49%	21.87%
1988	16.81%	17.45%
1987	5.23%	7.93%
1986	18.47%	48.49%
1985	32.16%	48.65%
Average Annualized Return	15.95%	18.14%

What they never seem to disclose, however, is that during that time the dollar was weak against most other major currencies. That weakness accounted for much of the performance superiority. So the performance advantage was due to a factor that could never persist over the long haul. In fact, it's more likely that over the long haul the market would neutralize that advantage. That's why you should be wary of short-term (less than ten years) comparisons. Twenty or thirty years gives a much more accurate picture of how market dynamics like currency fluctuations play themselves out.

IT'S A SMALL WORLD AFTER ALL—
IF YOU WANT QUALITY

Just because two-thirds of the world's stocks are non-U.S. companies does not mean there is a proportionally large pool of quality companies outside the U.S. One well-known fund manager once described most foreign companies as "dreck." To be sure, there are many great foreign stocks, but for every prince of a company a fund manager finds, he's got to kiss an awful lot of toads. The strongest, most innovative companies in almost every important market sector are dominated by U.S. names. Later in the book we'll talk about why that is, and whether it is likely to persist, but the current reality is clear. Since 1970, there have only been three years in which as many as 60% of the companies outside the U.S. outperformed the S&P 500. It has happened but once in the last twenty years! Yes, it's a great big *mediocre* investment world out there.

In the final analysis, the reality of the glamorous world of international investing looks pretty shabby. Foreign mutual funds are not likely to provide the low correlation characteristics that will add value to your portfolio. Neither are they likely to greatly enhance your absolute returns. They will, however, expose you to risks and volatility unlike anything you'll ever see here at home. Currency risk, political risk, liquidity risk—these are *added* risks that simply do not exist for investments here in the U.S. Next time a financial planner or columnist touts the benefits of "owning the world," you probably should reply, "Why in the world would I want that kind of grief?"

CHAPTER FOUR

IS VOLATILITY
THE SAME AS RISK?

THE CONVENTIONAL WISDOM in the investment world says that the more volatile an investment is, the riskier it is. Linking volatility with risk has become so commonplace that we never think to question whether it really is so. But question it we must, for it is *the single most damaging investment myth to which you will ever be exposed.*

So. Does volatility equate with risk? Yes, it does. And no, it doesn't.

Why the seeming contradiction? Because only when we establish the *time frame* for an investment can we make a reasonable judgment as to whether its volatility adds risk.

Let's assume that we have assembled a conventionally diversified portfolio with middle of the road allocations spread among all the usual asset classes: U.S., international, large company, small company, along with a healthy dose of bonds. Is this a risky portfolio? Maybe yes, maybe no. It all depends on the time frame context. If this were a portfolio designed to build a nest egg for a grandchild's college education fifteen years in the future, then yes, it would certainly be a low-risk strategy. There is little question that a decent pool of dollars will have accumulated and a high chance that the return would be considerably greater than that of a "risk-free" choice like a money market fund. On the other hand, if this sum of money were being put aside to use for a down payment on a house six months from now, that very same allocation would have to be termed extremely risky. There is no way of predicting with any degree of assurance how the markets will act over that short of a time frame. It is possible during that brief period for every asset in the portfolio to decline in value. There is not enough time to allow for your diversification to balance itself out, and not enough time to assure a window of opportunity to take profits at an appropriate time.

The rule is that the connection between volatility and risk *decreases* as the time frame *increases.*

The really fascinating element here is that over time, the conventionally expected dynamic actually reverses itself. Short term, volatile investments are riskier. Long term, stable investments are riskier. This is due to the fact that the greatest risk to long-term investors is inflation risk. Building capital to maintain and enhance one's future purchasing power is the primary concern for farsighted investors. Let's say we are investing for retirement and have a thirty-year time horizon. We can choose to put our money in a total market index fund and let it ride. In doing so, we will be exposed to a good deal of short-term volatility, but because our investment is basically tied to the growth of the economy over time, we are likely to finish with an acceptable return, particularly relative to inflation. We will have created genuine wealth.

Alternatively, we could choose to put all of our dollars into 90-day T-bills and regularly roll them over for thirty years. With this strategy, we would never expose ourselves to short-term volatility; our investment would be about as "safe" as could be. While we would have built a sizable pot of dollars, we would not have created much wealth. Our ability to build and maintain purchasing power using this "safe" strategy would be marginal at best. In fact, we could be putting the security of our retirement at risk due to our diminished purchasing power!

Viewing these concepts in this way helps us to more deeply understand the wisdom of some of the most successful investors. Warren Buffet, for example, has joked that his holding period is "forever." Not surprisingly, he is also famous for his disdain of those who obsess over short-term market moves. "As far as I'm concerned," he's said, "The stock market does not exist. It is there only as a reference to see if anybody is offering to do anything foolish."

If there is a fatal flaw in the advice of most mutual fund know-it-alls, it is to be found here, in assigning short-term risk labels to long-term investment options.

Financial planners and other assorted academically based practitioners make an interesting and compelling case for this seemingly senseless contradiction. "Not everyone," they say, "is a Buffet-like cool customer when it comes to market fluctuations. It's all well and good to talk long term, but what if the investor lets his emotions get the better of him, panics, and sells after the market has declined? We surely don't want that. Better to construct a more stable program that will allow the typical investor to stay the course and at least get some benefit from a long-term investment program."

I must admit the logic seems sound. Better half a loaf than none, eh? And I myself used variations on a similar theme for years to justify the fruit-salad portfolios I constructed. In the final analysis, though, it just doesn't hold up to careful scrutiny.

First of all, the underlying condescension implicit in this view is not only unappealing, it's simply wrong. "You, the investor, are a foolish knave. Left to your own devices you will react exactly opposite from how you should. I, the professional, will save you from yourself. Aren't you thankful you have the benefit of my wisdom and perspective?" Baloney. The reality, in more cases than we in the industry would like to admit, is just the opposite. (An inside joke in financial circles asks, "How can you tell the difference between a professional investor and an amateur? The professional panics first.") All of the data that I've seen seems to suggest that individual investors are getting more and more confident in staying the course in their investments during market storms. It's the pros, with their myriad tools and options, who seem to feel there is some imperative to make a move when the markets move.

The statistical reality is that only a very small percentage of investors make precipitous moves in times of turmoil. Yet the industry, in order to "protect" this very small minority, is poisoning the well for all investors. It is assumed anyone—everyone—will panic. So the assumption is that everyone should have that panic-proof portfolio. (Of course, we know there is no such thing as panic-proof equity allocation. When it hits the fan, all markets feel the pain.) Think of the waste! Think of all the dollars left on the table in this incredible bull market due to advisors with short-term mentalities and concerns "protecting" us from ourselves!

The industry would serve investors much better by expending more resources to educate that small minority of panic-prone individuals about the benefits of long-term perspectives rather than regularly touting "Moves You Need to Make Now!" (I know I'll hear from media folks who will insist that long-term investing is exactly what they preach to their readers. Yeah, right.

Your publications and programs scream urgency every day, every week, every month and you really believe the message investors get is to think long term? Who's kidding whom?)

It is these realities that make our approach to your portfolio so effective. I think it is safe to assume that the more one knows about an investment, the more likely one is to be comfortable with that investment. The strategy that we employ of investing in large U.S. companies leaves you with a portfolio of companies that you know: IBM, Microsoft, Intel, GE, Merck, Citigroup and the like. When times of crisis occur—as they inevitably will—you'll be dealing with investments you can understand. You'll own companies that are a part of the fabric of your life. You'll have a greater sense of confidence that the short-term fluctuations are not likely to mean much over the long term. This will greatly increase the odds that you will stay the course during market panics. That, as everyone knows, is more than half the battle. And we can't ever expect to win the battle for long-term investment excellence burdened by the volatility = risk straightjacket.

CHAPTER FIVE

THE DREAM TEAM FUMBLES

"Can't anybody here play this game?"
Casey Stengel, manager of the hapless 1962 Mets,
on viewing another terrible performance in a season
that set a record for ineptitude.

S URE, IT'S EASY TO CONSTRUCT, in the abstract, an argument critical of accepted practices. For all you know at
this point, I myself may have erroneously manipulated the data
to prove my point. (I haven't.) If you're inclined to think that
my criticisms may sound good on paper, but don't hold up in
the real world, get ready for a real shock. In the real world, it's
even worse than I've described.

Accountability is a pretty rare commodity in the fund advice
world. While there is no shortage of "experts" who, via the
media, will tell you what to buy and sell, what to look for and
what to avoid, it seems that their advice is rarely if ever revisit-
ed at a future date to see how good it was; that is, until *The New
York Times* began what has been the most fascinating and
instructive ongoing piece of financial journalism in this decade.

On July 7, 1993, *The New York Times* began a series that
reported on the advice of five mutual fund experts. Sheldon
Jacobs is the veteran editor of *The No-Load Fund Investor*, one

of the best mutual fund newsletters around. He also manages money for private investors. Harold Evensky is probably the best known name in financial planning. Author of numerous articles and books on a variety of financial topics, he also manages money for private investors. John Rekenthaler was, at the time the contest began, editor of *Morningstar Mutual Funds*, the single most looked-to source for information on funds. John left Morningstar in 1997 and was replaced in the *Times* series by Susan Dziubinski, editor of *Morningstar Investor*. (Rekenthaler has subsequently returned to Morningstar as its director of research but Dziubinski remains the Morningstar participant on the *Times* panel.) Jack Brill is an investment advisor in San Diego who specializes in "socially conscious" portfolios. Eric Kobren has a high profile in the fund world. He is editor of two successful newsletters, manages private money and runs two funds of funds. All told, a veritable "Dream Team" of mutual fund experts.

These experts were each given a hypothetical $50,000 to invest. They were instructed to create a long-term growth portfolio for someone with a twenty-year time horizon until retirement. The experts were free to use any funds they wished and were allowed to make changes in their portfolios quarterly. The *Times* has regularly reported on the opinions and strategies of these experts, and has chronicled changes made in the portfolios and the results achieved.

What a great journalistic idea this was! Here, in one place, investors would be able to see how five very different experts approach the task of constructing and managing an integrated portfolio of mutual funds. You would gain insights about real-life ongoing decision making and the results of those real decisions. You would see how experienced professionals, people who get paid good money to do this sort of thing, navigate the maze of the fund world and make (hopefully) superior selections based on years of experience and specialized industry knowledge.

But probably the most significant aspect of this project was that there was *follow-up:* We would get to see the results over time of decisions made. As simple as this sounds, it is quite unusual. The financial press inundates consumers daily with advice and recommendations from hundreds of experts and gurus. With the media focus on the here and now, there is little time, space or inclination to follow up to see just how that advice has done.

In *The New York Times* series we would finally get to see how experts react in real time to the ebbs and flows of the markets. How do they respond to crises? What do they do that you don't—and what might you learn from it?

Looking back over the last six years, a close analysis of the results, and how those results were created, confirms in no uncertain terms everything we've previously discussed.

The results the experts achieved ranged from marginally acceptable to downright disastrous.

Let me say right here that the purpose of this chapter is not to attack or embarrass any of the five participants. They are all intelligent, capable professionals who sincerely strive to do the best they can for investors. The reason this story needs to be told is to illustrate that the system is so flawed that even the best and the brightest cannot hope to achieve excellence within its confines.

On the surface, the results were not pretty. None of the five participants came close to besting the S&P 500. The best of the five broadly diversified portfolios made about 21% less than the S&P and the worst returned not much more than half of what the S&P did! Collectively, the average portfolio made only about 65% of what the S&P did. At first blush, we could see confirmation that diversifying away from large-cap U.S. stock funds did little but detract from overall returns.

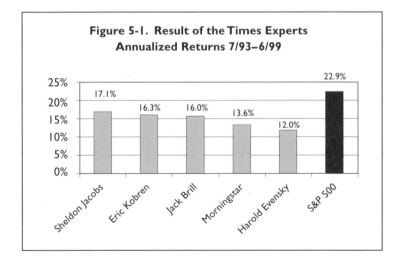

Figure 5-1. Result of the Times Experts
Annualized Returns 7/93–6/99

But wait a minute. That's not fair. These advisors all constructed diversified portfolios using funds from multiple asset classes that included small cap, international, emerging markets, real estate, and energy. So although the *Times* kept score using the S&P as a benchmark, we really should use a more apples to apples comparison. It is fairer to compare the experts' results to another broadly diversified approach. And that's when we begin to see the trouble in paradise. Because even when compared to a conventionally diversified mix of average funds, the experts' portfolios came up short. In most cases, far short.

We constructed a "neutral" mix that reflected as best as possible both the general form of the portfolios managed by the experts and prudent accepted conventional wisdom. We resisted the temptation to use 20/20 hindsight to stack the comparative model with the asset classes that have done the best over the past six years. Our neutral blend looked like this:

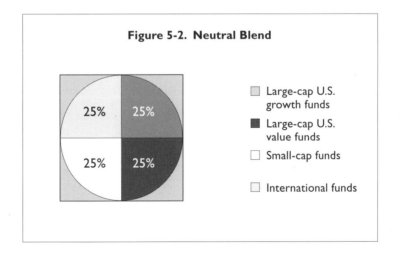

Figure 5-2. Neutral Blend

- Large-cap U.S. growth funds
- Large-cap U.S. value funds
- Small-cap funds
- International funds

We then took the return for the *average* fund in each of these categories over the six-year period and calculated what the "neutral blend" would have returned:

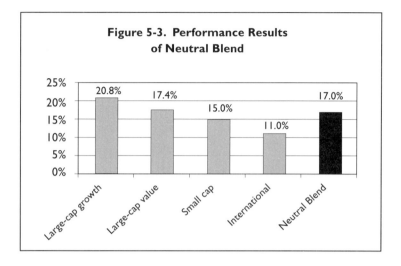

So we can see that the experts had a tough time beating the average fund in a neutral buy and hold blend over the six-year period.

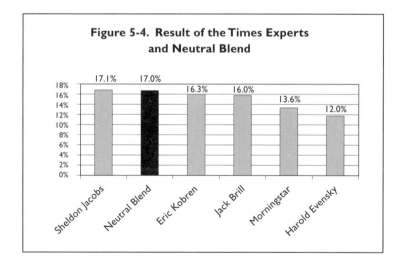

This is pretty significant—and damning—when we realize that we're talking about the *average fund*, not *market averages*. My guess is that each of the participants feels capable of picking better than average funds.

But what about risk? Most of the participants, in particular Harold Evensky, made frequent comments about keeping risk levels down and "sleeping at night." Perhaps the lower absolute returns (particularly in relation to the more narrowly focused S&P alternative) would look better if viewed with an eye to how well the portfolios held up during rough patches in the large-cap arena. This is the "bluff" that far too many financial planners try to pull off. Unfortunately, last year the market called the bluff. During the global crisis of 1998, the more broadly diversified portfolios simply didn't do the job from a stability standpoint.

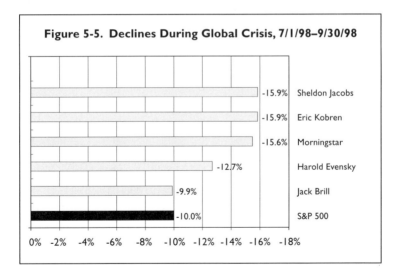

Figure 5-5. Declines During Global Crisis, 7/1/98–9/30/98

Now, maybe in the *next* big decline the virtues of diversification will be more apparent (this is the "wait 'til next year" gambit) but I'm not sure I like the odds. In any case, given the significant lag on the upside, the experts' portfolios would have to exhibit astonishing stability on the downside to arrive at anything close to a reasonable risk-adjusted return.

So what happened? Well, every expert labored within the flawed model we talked about in the beginning of the book. To varying degrees each of them:

◆ diversified among multiple asset classes,

◆ used Modern Portfolio Theory as a guide,

◆ hoped for outperformance from small caps,

◆ hoped for performance and risk reduction from international funds,

◆ confused risk with volatility, thus putting much short-term emphasis on what should have been a long-term approach,

and

◆ made numerous tactical moves in response to relatively short-term outlooks.

Perhaps it was due to the venue (a daily newspaper), but the *Times* experts regularly spoke of what they expected the market to do over the next several months, as if these short-term market moves were of great significance for a portfolio with a long-term time horizon. And while one could reasonably explain this as simply the language of daily financial journalism, it is telling that their actions supported their short-term perspective. *Not one of them ever went even one full year without making a trade.* With remarkably few exceptions, trades were made every quarter.

There were only eight times in six years when *any* of the five experts went as long as six months without a trade.

As I noted in the chapter on asset allocation and diversification, it is very hard to create value over time with frequent changes to a portfolio. And while Jacobs and Kobren did improve the return their original mix would have achieved, Evensky's trading cost him dearly. *Had he simply kept his original portfolio from July of 1993, he would now be in first place with a compound annual return of 17.56%.* Instead, his ongoing "analysis" and tactical changes put him in *last place* with a mere 11.99% annual gain.

I've often observed that the "smartest" investor can frequently be his own worst enemy. I don't think it is an accident that the Morningstar experts and Harold Evensky currently occupy the bottom two slots. My personal opinion is that they are probably the most knowledgeable and "sophisticated" of the group. As we've noted before, there is an almost irresistible tendency to use the tools that are available to you. When you're on the level of an Evensky or a Morningstar editor, you're talking about using a pretty complex and powerful arsenal of intellectual weapons. But more often than not, complexity is the enemy of the effective fund investor. As Warren Buffet said, "Business schools reward complex behavior more than simple behavior; but simple behavior is more effective." What we want to strive for is a fund portfolio that is sophisticated yet simple. Jacobs' and Kobren's techniques tend more toward that style; that may well be why they've done the best.

What is the only rational conclusion? That it is awfully difficult to find evidence that the diversified, tactically allocated approach to constructing and managing a fund portfolio works well in the real world. When we get five of the brightest practitioners all underperforming reasonable expectations, we've got to seriously question whether the paradigm itself is at fault. By now, the answer to that question should be obvious.

But where do go from here?

PART TWO

A RETURN TO SANITY

CHAPTER SIX

DELUSIONAL NO MORE: A REALITY-BASED APPROACH TO PRACTICAL PORTFOLIO MANAGEMENT

Patient: *Doctor, it hurts when I do this.* (patient raises his arm) *Can you tell me how to make it stop?*
Doctor: *Yes. Don't do that no more!*

Old vaudeville routine

LET'S REGROUP for a moment and see where we are. So far, we've casually trashed the hard work, extensive research, and sophisticated conclusions of a generation of Ph.D.s, Nobel Prize winners and other assorted brainiacs. Oh, well, all in a day's work.

Seriously, though, the important question still remains unanswered: Knowing now what causes the pain, how do we make it stop? Well, like the old vaudeville doctor advised, the first step is to *stop doing what doesn't work. We must reject the delusions that have been formulated over the past generation.*

DELUSION #1: It is delusional to use historic data to help determine how asset classes are likely to perform in the future.

Using historic data is doomed to failure. Even when the data are available in large and "clean" quantities, the odds of past patterns repeating into the future are so slim that relying on them significantly increases your risk. There is a good reason why investors are repeatedly told "Past performance is no guarantee of future results."

DELUSION #2: *It is delusional to believe that historic correlations have been accurately identified.*

Most historic correlations are nothing more than series' of random events. Just because someone has taken the trouble in hindsight to group certain events together does not prove a real and repeatable correlation.

DELUSION #3: *It is delusional to believe that small-cap stocks have historically outperformed large-cap stocks.*

This is the Big Lie of modern investing. Gross misunderstanding of real-life trading realities has led to an overly positive spin on small-cap performance. When "adjusted for reality," small caps have actually underperformed, while exposing investors to much higher volatility.

DELUSION #4: *It is delusional to believe that international diversification can predictably reduce volatility or increase returns.*

There is nothing in the historic record to indicate that this has ever been the case for long-term investors. A stronger case, in fact, could be made for just the opposite. In addition, as the global economy evolves and markets become more interconnected, the hope for non-correlated safe havens overseas becomes even more remote.

DELUSION #5: *It is delusional to believe that the ability to accumulate information makes that information "actable." It is also delusional to believe that tactical moves in reaction to shorter-term events create value either from an upside growth standpoint or a risk reduction perspective.*

The record is clear. Deviations from long-term strategies in reaction to shorter-term events are most likely to detract value from your portfolio. Remain constantly aware that the media does not and cannot differentiate between noise and important information. Do not let meaningless news filler impose short-term considerations on your long-term investments.

I recall the famous lines of Sherlock Holmes who said that, when attempting to solve a mystery, once one has eliminated all other options what one is left with is, no matter how strange it seems, probably the correct solution.

Let's apply that same reasoning: We know now that it makes little sense long term to own small-cap stock funds. We know now that it makes little sense long term to own international funds. We also know that active tactical asset allocation is likely to result in diminished results over time. What we are thus left with is simply:

1. Invest in U.S. stock funds,

2. Choose large-cap stock funds, and

3. Resist the temptation to trade.

Certainly this is a simple, easy-to-implement strategy. In the following chapters, we'll take a closer look at each of the assumptions and recommendations. We'll take a fresh and *forward-thinking* look at what the world is likely to do to our portfolios, and try to be objective about the pros and cons of this approach.

CHAPTER SEVEN

HOORAY FOR THE RED, WHITE AND BLUE CHIPS

"If I can't make money in a $5 trillion market,
it may be a little bit of wishful thinking to think
that all I have to do is get a few thousand miles away
and I'll start showing my stuff."
Warren Buffet

IT'S POSSIBLE—no, probable—that you're much better off keeping the equity portion of your portfolio right in your own backyard. This recommendation is the one that often meets with the greatest resistance, if not rage. In the December 1998 issue of *Money* magazine, fund columnist Jason Zweig observed, "If you've still got any money in mutual funds that invest outside the U.S., you're probably ready to shoot anyone who says that international investing is a good idea.... But the only people you should be itching to shoot are those who tell you *not* to invest overseas." (I guess I better ask Jason to check his six-shooter at the door next visit. In any case, Zweig's vehemence is better understood in light of the fact that, according to him, he's had some 40% of his portfolio overseas for the last several years. Ouch! That's gotta hurt.)

Nevertheless, the weight of the evidence makes it pretty difficult to refute the wisdom of an all-American strategy. As we've already seen, the historic record presents precious little evidence that foreign stocks have ever really added long-term value to a well-run U.S. portfolio. Then again, as we've warned previously, the historic record can be most misleading. Perhaps things have changed? And indeed they have—for the better! The position of the U.S. relative to the rest of the world is the best it has been in over forty years. And it's a good bet that this position won't change for some time to come.

Recently, two keen observers have weighed in on the big picture perspective regarding the current U.S. advantage: Thomas Friedman, foreign affairs columnist for *The New York Times* in his 1999 book, *The Lexus and the Olive Tree*,[2] and MIT economist Lester Thurow in his recent, *Building Wealth*.[3] Neither directly addresses the investment implications or gives specific investment advice, but they both conclude that, overall, the U.S. currently enjoys a competitive advantage of significant proportions. Neither they, nor I, would ever maintain that this will never change, but a quick overview of the nature of these advantages suggests that they are not ephemeral, nor are they likely to change anytime in the foreseeable future.

Advantage: U.S.

◆ Honest legal, regulatory and financial environment

◆ Ability to quickly allocate capital to new ideas

---

2 Thomas L. Friedman, *The Lexus and the Olive Tree* (New York: Farrar, Strauss and Giroux, 1999), pp. 297–305.

3 Lester C. Thurow, *Building Wealth: the New Rules for Individuals, Companies and Nations* (New York: HarperCollins, 1999)

- ◆ A culture that allows failure, embraces destruction and encourages creativity

- ◆ Flexible labor market and labor policies

- ◆ Openness to immigrants

- ◆ Superiority of U.S. secondary education

Individually, none of these points makes an economy superior. Collectively, they present a broad and deep case for strong American competitive advantage. Over time, companies that operate within this context will inevitably be in the best position to take advantage of growth opportunities. And, as night follows day, a strong economy with healthy underpinnings makes for the most productive investment environment. Let's take a closer look at each of these advantages with an eye toward how they help place American companies in a dominant position.

AN HONEST PLAYING FIELD

Of all the bounties we American investors benefit from, the abundance of honesty and fairness in our markets may be the most significant. And while these traits may not be necessary in the short run for strong economic performance, they are absolutely essential for the preservation and enhancement of any hard-won economic gains. Government corruption is so rare as to literally be a nonfactor in our business dealings. (Not so everywhere in the world.) The intricate web of legal safeguards that govern our financial markets creates a level of confidence and assurance that is essential to the efficient flow of capital.

The U.S. markets are the most *transparent* in the world; it's not difficult to see what is actually going on. From audited financial statements, to regulatory filings, to detailed earnings reports, we have the opportunity on an ongoing basis to access information vital to our decision making. Armed with that information, and assured of its accuracy, the market can then vote with its dollars, allocating more to and rewarding those who excel, and withdrawing from and punishing those who mismanage. Seen up close and short term it often looks messy, but it helps create an environment for sound and healthy long-term growth.

I don't think one can overestimate how important this all is. And how rare. In fact, one can make a case that every major economic crisis is ultimately rooted in deficiencies in honesty and disclosure. A lack of an honest regulatory and legal environment is toxic to healthy financial markets. Russia's current woes are clearly due to this. The Asian meltdown of 1997–98 could ultimately be traced to the house-of-cards mentality built by crony capitalism. Even Japan's woes in the 1990s, including its inability to seriously and decisively address its huge structural problems, are a direct result of secret and unethically cozy relationships fostered over decades between industry and government and special interest groups.

We are fortunate here in the U.S. to live in an era far removed from when we ourselves had to endure this "ethical trial by fire." The history of American finance previous to the 1930s is filled with one panic after another, caused almost inevitably by excesses that remained undetected for too long because of a lack of transparency and suitable regulation. No doubt we, too, would still be subject to that kind of unpredictability were it not for the flurry of post-crash legislation in the 1930s and '40s that created the firewall of regulation and oversight that now protects us all.

Certainly, there are foreign markets and economies with a

highly developed legal and regulatory environment. No one would compare Great Britain or Germany with Thailand and Korea. Even so, there is no other market where you'll find such rigorous public and private pressure to assure adherence to the "rules of the game" as in the U.S.

The integrity angle has been obscured by investors' joy in seeing freedom blossom around the world. Legendary investor and global investing pioneer John Templeton has remarked that freedom is the primary requisite for a market to prosper. He often eschewed placing dollars in certain markets because he felt the local government was too heavy handed and controlling. Templeton was, of course, right. What he, and his successors in emerging market investing, lost sight of (much to their shareholders' regret) was that freedom in the absence of rules for fair dealing ultimately leads to theft.

ABILITY TO QUICKLY ALLOCATE CAPITAL TO NEW IDEAS

Money in the U.S. sure moves fast these days. More often than not, we read of this in a negative context; i.e., Wall Street's unwillingness to look beyond this week's data release or next quarter's earnings expectation. No doubt there is a downside to the itchy, antsy, twitchy, can't wait quality of the U.S. markets. By the same token, we must acknowledge the benefits of our very fluid system. As Thomas Friedman observed, "Nothing is faster at throwing money at new ideas than American capital markets."

Sure, we scoff now at how Internet companies with no earnings are brought to market, raising hundreds of millions on only the haziest of business plans. But Microsoft, too, was once an IPO and for the past 10–15 years regularly has been derided as grossly overvalued. Inevitably, most of these new offerings will die a sure and quick death, costing investors dearly. Some, however, will grow, prosper, and create new businesses the likes of which we cannot even imagine today—businesses that will create enormous wealth for all of us. The system that allows that dynamic to exist and flourish is an invaluable, albeit messy, wealth creator. And its state-of-the-art form is to be seen only in the U.S.A.

Less visible to the general public, but no less important, is America's army of venture capitalists. Pure dollars aside, the astonishing depth of expertise the venture capital community brings to the all-important and fast-evolving high tech sector of our economy is invaluable. Here, again, the U.S. stands out from the rest of the world. Amazingly, according to Friedman, Massachusetts has a bigger venture capital industry than *all of Europe combined!* Want to make a bet on what country the next great technology companies are likely to be born?

Federal Reserve Chairman Alan Greenspan recently commented on how invaluable our highly developed and efficient capital markets are. The United States is preeminent in the strength and depth of both its banking system and capital markets. Businesses must have regular and efficient access to capital. The fact that we have two enormous systems—our banks and our bond markets—gives us what Greenspan referred to as a "spare tire." When circumstances cause turmoil in one, we can fall back to a great extent on the other. Few countries have this luxury, and it is rarely thought of as a vital ingredient to financial survival. Greenspan's apt metaphor was, "You don't notice the lack of a spare tire until you have a flat." The lack of depth in the capital markets of Asia was one of the things that contributed to the severity of their 1998 meltdown.

A CULTURE THAT ALLOWS FAILURE, EMBRACES DESTRUCTION AND ENCOURAGES CREATIVITY AND NEWNESS

In almost any human endeavor, it is difficult to achieve the highest potential without accepting the risk of possible failure. From sports, to the arts, to basic interpersonal relationships, we know that those who do not risk failure also never fully succeed. We rarely think about this in the economic sphere, but it is just as true there, too. One of the most remarkable American traits is our society's ability to be very success oriented while not overly penalizing failure. The entrepreneur who goes bankrupt and then rises once again to higher levels of success is a beloved cliché in the business world. Many in this country are amazed to find out that business failure carries an incredibly harsh stigma in many other developed countries. The greater level of negative judgment heaped upon those who fail in other countries is a strong *disincentive* to attempt new, potentially profitable, yet risky, endeavors.

From the very beginning, America was an entity resulting from the process of creating something new. From this "New World," a relatively small number of colonists willed into creation a nation that had never existed before. While the modern states of Japan, Germany, France, Great Britain, China and Russia are the result of centuries of slow evolution, America was created within the span of just a few generations—a relative blink of an eye. Not only that, the founders were attempting something that had never been done successfully before. A nation without a monarch? Who ever heard of such a thing? The conventional wisdom declared that such a setup was bound to descend into either anarchy or tyranny. With the benefit of two centuries of hindsight, we can be forgiven for thinking that our success as a nation was a certainty. In reality, the odds at the time were heavily stacked against us.

There has always been a strong strain of, "What the heck, let's go for it!" in the American character. I like to think that it's an inevitable characteristic of our collective gene pool. After all, this country was populated by those from all over the world who at one point said, "I want a change. I want to try something new. I'm willing to make that move." This character trait had to be incredibly strong for our immigrant ancestors to hazard the hardships and dangers needed simply to get here. And this is not just in our past. It continues to be a remarkable dynamic even today as immigrants from every corner of the globe pour into the U.S. The descendants of those who did not value newness, who did not lust for change, exist today also. They live in London, Tokyo, Warsaw, and Rome. And they are not creating the new, groundbreaking technologies and industries of the twenty-first century.

But newness and change rarely occur in isolation. They most likely involve the destruction or leaving behind of the old. Capitalism has been described as a process of "creative destruction." In the constant struggle of the marketplace, companies find room to grow by pushing aside and subsuming others that haven't as much to offer and are not strong enough to resist. This process regularly renews and energizes the economic landscape, clearing dead wood and inefficient players.

The story of the United States has, throughout its existence, been one of destruction and creation. No doubt this urge has been at the core of some of the least attractive aspects of U.S. history and culture: The virtual extermination of indigenous cultures in the rush to expand westward is one manifestation.

The sometimes manic urge to tear down the old (as in buildings) in order to build anew is another, more benign example. (Minneapolis, where I live, is a textbook example of urban destruction run amuck; standing in the middle of downtown, one could easily assume that the city did not exist before 1960 because so many older structures have been torn down.)

In the economic sphere, however, there is an ongoing measure of accountability that keeps the process of destruction and rebuilding from becoming a negative dynamic. If it isn't working, if the benefits are not manifest, the process simply won't continue. So the willingness to "destroy," to tear down so that something new can be constructed is not only a positive trait, it is absolutely essential to the workings of capitalism. I firmly believe that it is this aspect of our national character that has enabled us to overcome obstacles (many self-created) and work through crises while our peers in Europe and Japan stay stuck in old methods and paradigms.

FLEXIBLE LABOR MARKETS/POLICIES

America's ability to make maximum use of human capital gives us a strong advantage as we move into the knowledge-based economies of the twenty-first century. Our flexibility is unique in that it is a flexibility of both management and labor. There is no other developed market of our size where labor has so many options. If things get tough in the Northeast, it is fairly easy for families to relocate to another section of the country where jobs and opportunities are greater. A move from Boston to Phoenix is relatively simple. Same language. Same currency. Same political and social systems. Compare this to Europe. If times are tough in Stockholm, it is not a very practical option to simply pick up the family and relocate to Barcelona. Talk all you want about European integration, but the reality is that, other than at the highest executive level, the labor market is not very liquid. Asia is even worse. It is simply not an option for the Thai factory worker to relocate to Japan for a better job. America's ability to shift labor resources quickly and efficiently to where they are needed and where the opportunities lie helps to maximize the growth potential in our economy.

Likewise, there is no other democratic society where management has as much flexibility to allocate labor resources efficiently. To put it bluntly, it's pretty easy to fire workers here in the U.S. Is that a bad thing? In the context of the big picture, no. The ability of management to downsize to help save a company during rocky periods is absolutely essential. Unfortunately, the short-term pain that these actions create is what inevitably gets the big press headlines. But we've also seen during the past decade that the ability to downshift also frees up management to *hire* as well. Fact is, if you can't fire someone, you'll think twice about hiring someone. Contrast our practices in this area to those of Japan and Europe, where layoffs are rare and difficult to execute. Is it any surprise that during the decade where we have created an enormous number of new jobs, employment in the rest of the developed world has stagnated?

OPENNESS TO IMMIGRANTS

It has always been, and always will be, our country's ultimate secret weapon. And of all of our advantages, this is the single one that is likely never to be overcome by our global competition. Germany, France, Japan, China, et al. would literally have to change how they view themselves as nations to establish the kind of open door we have. And that's not likely to happen. So for the indefinite future, we alone get to issue invitations to the best and brightest from around the world. We are regularly replenished with new waves of enthusiasm, hopes, excitement, and willingness to strive upward.

Certainly, it's not a steady progress, and sometimes we have to pause to catch our breath. But that underlying fermentation caused by the regular infusion of the new into the old is at the heart of America's ability to regularly reinvent itself to meet new challenges. As Jack Paar once said, "Immigration is the sincerest form of flattery."

SUPERIORITY OF U.S. UNIVERSITIES

Admittedly, any discussion of education here in the U.S. must confront some dizzying contradictions. At the same time that we are engaged in a huge national debate about the quality and results of K–12 education, our universities are the envy of the world. In a fast-evolving, knowledge-based economy, this is just one more advantage we enjoy. When the brightest from France, India, and China come to study here, many inevitably stay. Their high-level skills are then put to use building and expanding the U.S. economy. This must be maddening to our global competitors. Think how we would feel if many of our best computer and science students went to Germany or India to study and then stayed on to work for foreign companies.

The attraction of our institutions of higher learning is an outgrowth of much of what we have already discussed about the nature of the U.S. There is an openness, a willingness to question the old and embrace the new in our educational institutions that is often lacking overseas. Whether it is verbalized or not, students looking for the ticket to twenty-first century success know that it's more likely to get punched at an American university.

THE JAPAN ANALOGY

Inevitably in these discussions someone will rise and gravely say, *"Ah, I remember only ten years ago that everyone thought Japan had the answer to all the economic questions. We all thought Japanese companies would dominate the world and that we here in America would not be able to compete with their onslaught. So if you were writing this book back then, you probably would have recommended that we put all our money in Japan. Ha! Look at what happened. They've crashed while we soared. That just goes to show you how dangerous your reasoning is."*

Baloney.

Don't fall for that revisionist story about how everyone thought Japan was so great ten years ago. The reality is just the opposite. The only people who were bullish on Japan were either folks who had no knowledge of economics or those with a political or social agenda that needed an omnipotent Japanese "bully" to use as a foil. Most clear-eyed observers knew the situation to be laughably unsustainable. Admittedly, no one could really tell how long the craziness would last, but we all knew it was crazy. Price earnings ratios of 70 and above for *mature* companies were explained not by expectations of future dynamic growth, but by the lame reasoning that "Japanese accounting is different." You think we're in a bubble? Here's a real bubble, Japanese style: At one point, the grounds of the Imperial Palace in Tokyo were valued greater than all the real estate in California! So don't try to tell me that we're headed for the same kind of hubris-induced fall that Japan had. It just doesn't fly.

I'll be the first to say that we don't want to be so wrapped up in the red, white and blue that we lose sight of the reality that things can change. Not all of the advantages we've explored will persist forever. And even with those advantages, there is no guarantee that the U.S. market will always perform strongly. In fact, I can guarantee that it won't. I hope we can accept that the message is not that black and white. What is very clear, however, is that we do possess as a nation a number of significant competitive advantages. These advantages not only help us in good times, but they contribute to our ability to "right the ship" when things go wrong. I can only conclude that, given the weight of these advantages over time, investment results here in the U.S. will stack up well against any other global alternative.

CHAPTER EIGHT

BIGGER IS BETTER

*"The race does not always go to the swift, nor
the battle to the strong—but that's the smart way to bet."*
Damon Runyon

A S WE'VE ALREADY SEEN, the evidence is conclusive that there
is no small-cap advantage; in fact, when accurately adjusted, the data tend to point to large caps as the better performers
over time. Nevertheless, that alone would not and should not be
a reason to have large caps dominate your portfolio. *The more
important question is what to expect in the future.* Can we know
the future for sure? Of course not. Still, it is childish to simply
say that we cannot/should not choose just because we cannot
know the future for absolute certain. It is possible to examine the
world as it is currently ordered and attempt to come to some
simple conclusions regarding how things may unfold down the
road. And while we never achieve 100% accuracy, it certainly is
reasonable to make judgments based on the weight of the evidence that appears in front of us.

As I have gone through that process I have concluded that, as
a group, large company stocks are likely over time to deliver
superior performance over small company stocks. The returns

for investors concentrating on a large-cap strategy will be higher on an absolute basis and the accompanying volatility is likely to be less. Among the many reasons, several stand out:

◆ Large companies have greater material, financial and human resources, giving them a competitive advantage in a global economy.

◆ Large companies have advantages in marketing.

◆ Large companies have advantages in R&D.

◆ Large companies have advantages in management skills.

◆ Large-cap mutual funds are not subject to growth disadvantages like small-cap funds.

◆ Large-cap mutual funds get to hold winners indefinitely and are not hampered by artificial size constraints.

COMPETITIVE ADVANTAGE IN A GLOBAL ECONOMY

As we've previously noted, the big winners in the years to come will be those companies whose operations are widely distributed within the global economy. The lion's share will inevitably go to businesses that maximize return on a worldwide basis. There's nothing new or radical or starry eyed about this. It is simply the continuation of a trend that had been in place for a hundred years. The nineteenth century economy was dominated by local and regional companies or "brands." As new technologies of communication, transportation, manufacturing and storage were developed, *national* brands began to develop and eventually dominate. Now, the idea of a company prospering on a primarily local or regional basis seems almost quaint. It may find a way to survive, but it is unlikely to remain a long-term money machine. Certainly it will not be looked on with great favor by the financial markets. It is almost a given that any reasonably-sized operation will now consider itself national in some way.

We now find ourselves in the beginning stages of the *globalization* of brands and services, with leading-edge companies working the global market. Ford, Citigroup, Intel, GE, Coke, Microsoft, Nike, et al. are the brands of choice from Boston to Bangkok.

The transition from local to national, while helping to create some enormous new economic entities, was pretty hard on many small local and regional businesses. Many of those that weren't bought out or destroyed remain as just a shell of their former vital selves. Even so, the transition from local to national was a cakewalk compared with the tasks facing companies that now want or need to compete on a global basis. In the past, a company in the Midwest could expand nationally with relatively limited added resources. But to expand internationally brings a host of issues/problems that never existed before. Language differences. Currency differences. Culture differences. Distances that make Chicago to Boston seem like a walk in the park.

Sure, we can all talk about how technology and the Internet are allowing even small fry to act like big fish, but in the real world of global business, the companies with the biggest and best resources usually end up the winners. Human resources. Material resources. Financial resources. It may tickle our sense of justice to think of the underdog battling and defeating the big guy, but when the rubber meets the road, *size matters*.

Just as the trend toward national economies didn't mean the death of local and regional companies, the trend toward a global economy doesn't mean that national brands can't be fine businesses and great investments. Our only point is that the big, broad trend of history is not on the side of those who aren't growing globally. Financial markets invariably, over time, reward most those companies that show the greatest growth in their niche. The global marketplace is the only place to achieve that level of sustained growth.

The global marketplace, however, is not without its risks, as was abundantly demonstrated in 1998. Yet even then we saw that it was the small and mid-size companies that often suffered the most. These were companies that had "gone global" but did not have a broad enough global presence. They were far too dependent on the fortunes of a single country or region. They were not large enough to have truly diversified global operations and thus felt a larger proportional impact from the Asian meltdown. Contrast this with the balance shown by a company like Intel, whose revenues [as of the first quarter of fiscal year (FY) 1999] were broken down from these sources: North America 42%; Europe 28%; Asia-Pacific 22%; Japan 8%.

OTHER OVERALL COMPETITIVE ADVANTAGES

Rare is the company that can prosper long without substantial efforts expended in research and development. Here, again, the differences between large and small are compelling. Since we just mentioned Intel, we might look at its research and development (R&D) expenditures. In FY1998, Intel pumped over *$2.6 billion* into R&D. Incredible. The size of the pool of dollars alone is only part of the picture. Equally important is the fact that this larger pool enables companies to spread out into areas that a smaller pool would not allow. A more diverse R&D effort not only reduces risks, it also increases the chance of hitting on that new idea, process or product that helps feed future growth.

Large companies also sport advantages in marketing. Whether it's getting your message out or distributing your product where you need it when you need it, it's tough to compete against the biggest.

An often-overlooked area in which large companies can claim an advantage is management. Quality, innovative management is a major key to the success of any company in this global economy. Many of the fund managers we work with look at management as one of the top factors that will affect their decision on taking a position in a stock. I do not think it unreasonable to assume that in this case, like so many others, the "cream rises to the top." The best corporate managers, the ones who are the most visionary, the most able to make things happen, will inevitably end up playing in the big leagues. The challenge of success in the global arena, not to mention the incredible potential financial rewards, attracts the best and the brightest. The Jack Welches of the world (the legendary leader of GE) don't stay long undiscovered in small and medium-sized companies. Success with a small company quickly leads to bigger challenges with larger companies. So even in the more difficult to quantify areas of management and leadership, a strong case could be made that you wouldn't want to bet against the big guys.

BIG CAP CO-OPTATION

Looking for the new little company that's getting ready to knock one of the big guys off its perch? Dream on. Sure, it may happen once in a blue moon, but the more likely scenario is that the big company will simply buy the smaller company. You see this in the news on an almost weekly basis. The story goes like this: small company develops innovative new technology; knowledgeable insiders recognize the value/danger this represents; dominant company in sector then buys little company and exploits the new technology.

THE INVESTMENT ANGLE

Conventional wisdom says that one of the reasons investment opportunities are greatest in small caps is because they are followed less by Wall Street, thus making it more likely that one can do diligent research and uncover a truly undiscovered gem. On the surface, this notion is intriguing. Find that diamond in the rough and wait for the rest of the market to recognize its brilliance. Unfortunately, reality doesn't often confirm this faith.

I suppose at one time there may have been something to this idea. These days, though, it's difficult for quality companies to remain undiscovered for very long. The scrutiny in this area is intense. Money managers regularly use the powerful computer resources available to them (not available a generation ago) to screen thousands of possibilities on a regular basis. Every potential angle is explored. Anything that looks the least bit promising will be followed up. The follow-up is simpler, too, on the small company. It is a lot easier for an analyst to fully comprehend the situation with a small company than with the often more diversified and complex operations of a large company.

What I find fascinating, and many find surprising, is that in reality the largest "best known" companies are actually *underfollowed and/or underanalyzed* by Wall Street. In fact, the conventional wisdom that everything there is to know is already known about big companies is a myth. Vanguard in late 1997 did a study that looked at what the large institutions on the Street were actually buying. What they found was that mutual funds, which control some 22% of the country's stocks, owned just over 13% of the 100 largest companies in the U.S. and over 34% of companies that ranked 901 to 1000. These latter companies had market caps that ranged from $600 million to $1.1 billion: small-cap territory.

The research showed that actively managed funds owned just 4% of Coca-Cola, 6% of Exxon, 7% of Microsoft, 9% of GE, and only 9% of Merck and 14% of Intel. (Remarkably, Warren Buffet's Berkshire Hathaway owns more than twice as much Coke *as the entire fund industry.*)

There seems to be a clear bias among the big, "smart" money *against* big companies. Everyone, it seems, is looking for that undiscovered gem among the smaller issues. Even among brokerage firm analysts, the dynamic remains the same. Research has shown that there is a decided lack of coverage among the fifty or so largest stocks. Some had absolutely no coverage and for many, no recent reports had been generated.

In-depth analytical coverage of large companies is not nearly as great as one would expect. In classic counter-intuitive fashion, a strong case could be made that it is among the largest companies that savvy analysts may find their skills best used. Large-cap managers have told us on numerous occasions that Wall Street regularly misunderstands what goes on with some of the largest stocks. A large company with numerous subsidiaries and operations across different businesses can be difficult to interpret. Analysts and managers who stay within the small-cap arena are, in many ways, taking the easier and simpler way out. The huge multinational is the tough nut to crack. If you can do it, not only can you get a leg up on the competition, but the rewards can be large and sustainable.

THE BURDENS OF SMALL-CAP FUNDS

Even if we believed that small caps would perform well over time, small cap mutual funds are among the worst long-term holdings an investor could choose. If they stay true to their asset class, they are doomed to mediocrity.

The ultimate flaw in small-cap investing, its genetic defect if you will, is that a successful small cap doesn't remain a small cap for long. Here's the reality: Let's say we are managing a small-cap fund. Our median market cap is around $800 million (the median market cap of the small-cap funds tracked by Morningstar). We own a stock that turns out to be a real winner. It doubles. It now has a market cap of $1.6 billion. We're now out of small-cap territory and into mid-cap levels. It rises another 50% and we're now sitting on a company with a market cap of almost $2.5 billion. By any measure, this is no longer a small cap. We now have two choices. We can sell the stock, since it no longer qualifies as a small cap, thus remaining true to our fund's charter. But that's kind of like uprooting your roses and letting your weeds continue to grow.

We could, alternatively, fudge our objectives and rationalize that even though this is no longer a small-cap stock, it was small when we bought it, so we'll hang on for as long as seems wise. While that may well be the best choice from a pure investment standpoint, we cannot ignore the fact that by doing so we are now no longer investing in small caps. We have mid caps, perhaps even some large caps in the portfolio.

Essentially, we're damned if we do, damned if we don't. If we keep *selling our successes*, we place an incredible burden on ourselves to constantly replace otherwise good investments. If we don't sell, we end up managing something far different than a small-cap fund.

Contrast this dilemma with the freedom a large-cap fund has. The large-cap fund can let its winners ride indefinitely. They never become too large. We can thus benefit from Peter Lynch's proverbial "ten bagger," the stock that goes up five- or ten-fold over an extended period.

Small-cap funds are almost always ruined by success. It does not take long in this era of intense media scrutiny and quest for short-term performance for a good record to attract lots of dollars. But the larger a small-cap fund becomes, the more positions it must take to fill the portfolio. Or, it must start to buy larger and larger companies. Either way, the dynamic that created the initial success is destroyed. Growth of assets is the kiss of death for a small-cap fund, making it senseless as a long-term holding. Funds that invest in large companies, on the other hand, don't have that problem. There is very little difference between investing $500 million in large caps as opposed to $5 billion in large caps. The size and liquidity of large caps enable managers to handle huge sums with relatively little difficulty. Certainly far less difficulty than that of the small-cap manager. There are numerous examples of small-cap funds that have suffered lagging performance after doubling and tripling their assets. And there are just as many large-cap funds whose performance has remained excellent after equivalent asset gains. Bottom line is that if you're a long-term investor, you're better off picking a fund that you can realistically hold long term.

I repeat to those who continue to believe that the large-cap U.S. strategy is based on simply chasing "what has worked recently:"

Even in the absence of recent strong large-cap performance, a reasonable observer could still conclude—going forward—that large-cap stocks have inherent and undeniable advantages over their smaller cousins. And those advantages are likely to persist for quite some time.

CHAPTER NINE

GROWTH VS. VALUE

So far, we've determined that our chances for long-term success are greatest here in the U.S. We've also concluded that the odds favor large-cap stock funds over small-cap funds. But we're not done yet; there still remains one more important decision to make. Not all large-cap funds are alike. There are two broad categories of large-cap funds, *growth* funds and *value* funds. They each reflect a particular style of stock selection. And the degree to which we allocate between the two could have a major impact on our results.

So what's the difference between growth and value, and why is the distinction so important? Managers who are growth investors usually look to earnings as their primary focus. The philosophy is that stock prices ultimately follow earnings. As earnings grow, so too should the price of the stock. Typically, growth-fund managers will seek to find companies that they believe are or will be experiencing rapid and sustained increases in revenues and profits, with the expectation that those increases will translate into soaring earnings.

The typical value investor scoffs at this method, feeling there is too much "pie in the sky" built into the process. Value investors tend to be more practical, contrarian, bargain-hunting types. They look for companies they believe to be unfairly treated by Wall Street and whose stock prices are thus temporarily depressed. Companies they like will tend to be "cheap" as measured by some standard valuation criteria like PE, book value, or some other historic norm. (PE equals the price per share divided by the earnings per share, usually on a trailing twelve-month basis.)

Value investors invariably opt for the bird in hand; growth investors are comfortable betting there are two in the bush.

It is an ongoing conversation in the investment world as to which style of stock picking is "best." There have been periods when Growth was king, and times when Value was clearly the winner. Many observers note that since value investors are already buying assets that have been beaten down, the consequences of being wrong are not as severe. They thus claim that a value-driven strategy is inherently less risky. Most financial planners, with their bias toward appearing "thoughtful and prudent" will tend to overweight value in their portfolio recommendations. The fact remains, though, that the longer the time frame we examine, the more it appears—historically—that there has been very little difference in the long-term returns. When the dust has settled, it's pretty much a statistical dead heat. So far.

As we've said over and over again, however, we should be wary of placing too much weight on conclusions based on historic returns. Things change. Therefore, while the long-term stats might dictate a more or less equal weighting between growth and value, this may not be the wisest course going forward. There is a wild card in the deck, and you don't want to play your hand until you've taken it into account. *The wild card is technology.*

I am in the camp that believes technology is having, and will continue to have, a transformational impact on our lives. In all spheres—social, political, economic—the ordering of the world is in the process of being radically changed. An increasingly larger and larger percentage of the U.S. economy's growth each year is directly attributable to technology. One of the few sure bets for the next twenty years is that the largest and most successful companies will be those that create and take advantage of new technologies. Investors who resist this risk are missing the greatest wave of growth they will ever get to see.

To be sure, with these tremendous opportunities come significant risks. I have a pretty good idea that Coca-Cola will be profitably bottling caramel-colored fizzy water thirty years from now. I'm not as sure I'll be buying "Windows 2028" from Microsoft. (That's Warren Buffet's famous tech-avoidance line of reasoning.) And we can't deny that there are probably an awful lot of technology companies with stratospheric PEs that are destined to crash and burn. But the concerns of the tech-nervous aren't really anything new or particularly perceptive. Sure, over the past twenty years there have been plenty of "leaders" who eventually became extinct footnotes. Plenty of high fliers that crashed and burned. Plenty of "pies in the sky" that were more hype than substance. *Yet when all was said and done, with all the ups and downs, euphoria and despair, technology stocks have returned more than any other sector.* Creative destruction is the name of the game in the world of twenty-first-century technology investing. So yes, there is great short-term uncertainty in technology investing. But those who are willing and able to accept this *short-term uncertainty* receive in return greater *long-term certainty* of excellence.

The problem for the value camp is that a good number of value managers can't—or refuse to—make this "leap of faith." Technology companies are by their nature dynamic, rapid growers.

Their stocks almost invariably are tagged as growth stocks. When we see how value investors view the world, and how they judge the worth of stocks, it's no wonder that few technology companies show up in their portfolios. Currently the average large-cap value fund has about a 9% weighting in technology, less than half the tech weighting in the S&P 500. I can't help but think that it's going to be pretty hard to capture the dynamic of the twenty-first-century economy with such marginal participation in its most dynamic sectors.

With that in mind, an equal weighting between growth and value is certainly not the most productive strategy. Funds that have a growth orientation, as opposed to a value slant, should dominate your portfolio. And those growth funds should overweight technology. This could increase your portfolio's short-term volatility (although we may be surprised down the road to find that large technology stocks were, in fact, not as volatile as we imagined them to be). But remember, we have already decided to free ourselves from the artificial constraint that equates volatility with risk. In reality, positioning your portfolio to more accurately reflect the economic landscape in the future is probably less risky than clinging to notions that may not be relevant to the world ahead.

Does that mean that we *totally* reject value-oriented strategies? By no means. Many excellent companies fall within this category. I am positive, for example, on financial services companies, many of which fall within most value managers' comfort range. So I have and continue to own certain value funds in my clients' portfolios. We simply own a much smaller percentage than most advisors currently recommend.

Having said all that, I would be remiss if I didn't acknowledge that there are many observers who question whether we should make a sharp distinction between growth and value. And the truth is, the dividing line is more than a bit hazy at times. Depending on what part of the economic cycle we find ourselves in, typical growth stocks may find themselves in value portfolios and vice versa. In addition, there really isn't one monolithic value style. These days a value fund may be one, like The Oakmark Fund, that almost completely avoids the usual tech suspects. Or it may be a fund like Legg Mason Value that has benefited enormously from recent large positions in soaring tech stocks like AOL and Dell. There's no question that Oakmark manager Robert Sanborn's definition of value is a good deal different from that of Legg Mason's manager, Bill Miller.

My feelings are this: I'm open to the potential benefit of having a value fund in my portfolio. I prefer, however, that my value manager not be dogmatically opposed to technology. Not every tech stock sports an astronomical PE. When values are there, I expect my value manager to be farsighted enough to recognize them and move on it.

The exact allocation between growth and value in any given portfolio depends, in the final analysis, on the individual investor's goals, time frame, and personal preferences. I hesitate to assign a specific "best" allocation. (Remember, there's no such thing as the "Efficient Frontier.") Suffice it to say the bottom line is that for the long-term investor, growth should definitely take precedence over value.

CHAPTER TEN

HOW TO TAILOR THIS STRATEGY TO FIT YOU

U P 'TIL NOW, we've focused on how to achieve the most productive *equity* portfolio. But not everyone wants his or her entire portfolio exposed to the market. In most cases, an investor will allocate at least some assets to bonds or money markets for any number of perfectly rational reasons. Perhaps you are looking at a relatively short time frame, where market volatility could have a significant impact on your potential for success. Obviously, dollars that you will need in 2–3 years should not be totally exposed to market volatility. The risk of needing them when the market is down may be too great. Or perhaps you have a long time horizon but your need for growth is not particularly great and is exceeded by your desire for regular calm and serenity in your financial life. If you are in the fortunate position where a return of 7–8% a year will give you more money than you will ever reasonably need over time, you may question why you should expose your entire portfolio to market volatility. In these and other circumstances, it is certainly appropriate to diversify away from large-cap U.S. growth funds.

But remember that our cardinal rule remains the same: *Never use one equity asset class to hedge against another equity asset class. If you want to reduce the volatility inherent in a large-cap U.S. stock fund strategy, only bonds and cash should be used.*

DIVIDING YOUR PORTFOLIO

Executing our strategy is extremely simple. Your portfolio will be divided into two parts. One part will be your equity allocation. This portion will provide the significant growth potential to your portfolio and will also expose your portfolio to short-term volatility. The other part will be your bond/money market allocation. This portion won't contribute much to your potential growth over time, but will act as a short-term stabilizer in the portfolio.

Asset allocation	Return potential	Short-term volatility
Large-cap U.S stock funds	high	high
Bonds/Cash	low	low/none

How you mix these two asset classes together depends on what volatility/return dynamic you wish to create. As you layer in more bonds and money market funds, you will reduce your short-term volatility and also reduce your long-term return potential. When we map this out on paper, the graph looks like this:

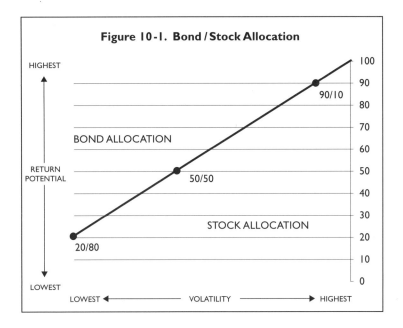

The Volatility/Return Trend Line

But wait a minute! This looks suspiciously like the Efficient Frontier that I've previously labeled as bogus financial voodoo. Am I contradicting myself? No. Recall that the major flaw in the Efficient Frontier model was the assumption that one could determine what the future correlations between various equity asset classes would be. In other words, you had to believe that you could know what both the volatility and return relationships would be among U.S., International, large cap, small cap, etc., well into the future. We realize now that is simply impossible.

It *is* possible, though, to know how a money market fund will react to any stock market situation. *Its reaction is always the same.* Every day of every year for your entire investment life, the money market portion of your portfolio will be earning a small but steady rate of interest, with the principal always rock steady.

So you know exactly how this allocation will affect your overall portfolio. You know for a fact that when the market is strong, your cash allocation will be a drag on performance. You also know for a fact that when the market is plummeting, your cash allocation *will* perform as a stabilizer. There will be no surprises.

This "no surprise" quality is what differentiates this method of asset allocation from the typical Modern Portfolio Theory Efficient Frontier voodoo. In an investment world that is filled with uncertainty, this quality of *predictability* is of tremendous value.

It also forces you as an investor to honestly confront the degree to which you wish to assume market volatility. As we've mentioned before, the only way to avoid market volatility is to avoid the market; the only way to reduce market volatility is to reduce your exposure to the market. You cannot reduce market volatility with any reasonable degree of assurance by substituting one equity class for another.

One important point to note is that since we are relying on one part of the portfolio for certain and ongoing stability, our choices will be limited. Many of the bond fund options that are normally recommended simply will not pass muster. Remember that bonds are sensitive to interest rate moves and will decline in value when interest rates rise. So most bond funds won't offer the assurance of stability we need for our model. Thus, in addition to money market funds, the only bond funds that should be used to execute this strategy would be high quality bond funds that hold bonds with very short maturities. In most cases, with proper selection, they can offer a bit higher return than a money market option with only minimal addition of volatility.

The good news in all this is that the added assurance of stability in our bond/money market allocation allows us to have a slightly larger allocation to equities without sacrificing short-term stability. Thus, over the long haul, we are likely to see greater returns.

CHAPTER ELEVEN

"IF YOU'RE SO SMART, HOW COME MY FINANCIAL PLANNER SAYS YOU'RE CRAZY?" (AND OTHER QUESTIONS YOU'RE TOO POLITE TO ASK)

I'M CONSTANTLY AMAZED at the remarkable power of cherished dogma to withstand the assault of facts. There is a quasi-religious belief in the concepts we've shown to be false that causes otherwise intelligent professionals to often half listen, hearing only those snippets that fit into their preconceived notions of how the world works.

I want you to be able to use the information in this book to help create a better investment program. In doing so, you may face members of the dogmatic old guard who will twist facts and take data out of context in order to defend their positions and bully you into staying on the wrong track.

To help you stand your ground I've put together a "devil's advocate" question and answer section that addresses the objections of someone stuck in the old ways. You'll see how each and every criticism of our approach is grounded less on facts and more on half-truths, misunderstandings, and false suppositions. You may even teach your financial planner a thing or two, for when facts are joined with common sense, the result is very powerful.

OBJECTION: So you're simply saying that I should move all my money into large-cap U.S. growth stocks. It sure looks like you're just chasing what's been hot lately. You criticize asset allocators for doing the same thing with small portions of their portfolios, yet here you are betting the ranch by doing the same thing with your entire portfolio.

ANSWER: First, let's be clear that I don't think everyone should have his or her entire portfolio in large-cap U.S. growth stocks. As I made clear in chapter 10, many investors will choose to add bonds or money markets to the portfolio in order to create a mix they are comfortable with. But yes, of the long-term growth portion of your portfolio, large-cap U.S. stock funds are the way to go. It is incorrect, however, to think we like large-cap U.S. stock funds simply because they have done well recently. I regularly caution investors not to put too much weight on historic returns. Things change. You'll note that throughout the book, we only use historic return data to demonstrate that the dogmas of the asset allocators have never produced effective results in the real world. It wasn't until we looked forward at who and what is most likely to benefit from trends that currently exist and are likely to persist for some time that we concluded large-cap U.S. stock funds was the place to be. I can't stress strongly enough that our strategy is *forward looking and long-term oriented*.

OBJECTION: Everything I read says that small-cap stocks outperform large caps over the long run. How can you be right and everyone else wrong?

ANSWER: What can I say? Facts are facts. The fact is the data that was used to "prove" the superiority of small caps is incredibly flawed. If you're promoting small-cap performance and are not aware of the dynamics of the return numbers during the 1930s and '40s you ought to admit you don't know what you're talking about. Simply repeating bad analysis over and over won't make it true. What is even more scandalous is that most of the thoughtful people in the industry know this. But they so want to believe the small-cap myth that they do their best to ignore the flaws in the data.

Of course, the fact that small caps have not outperformed large caps over the long haul does not mean that they can't or won't over the next 75 years. But I'd like to have you explain to me, given the emerging global dynamic, how that is likely to happen. The sad fact is, you like small caps because you've been brainwashed to think they have outperformed substantially in the past. Eliminate the comfort that dogma gives you and all you're left with is a risky, underperforming asset class. Do you really want to put a substantial chunk of your portfolio there?

QUESTION: You talk a lot about the global economy. Isn't it true that more than half the companies in the world are outside the U.S.? How can you just dismiss them? Aren't there a lot of great companies in other countries to invest in?

ANSWER: You're right. There are a lot of great companies overseas. But our large-cap strategy doesn't preclude investing in them. Most large-cap U.S. stock funds will at various times own some of the best foreign companies. Funds I currently invest in own or have owned foreign companies such as Nokia, Philips, SAP, Royal Dutch, Hong Kong Telecom, Smith-Kline Beecham,

Sony, Schlumberger, Volkswagen and UBS, just to name a few. I like that my large-cap U.S. stock funds managers can pick and choose the cream of the foreign universe. But cherry picking a select few is far different than trying to find dozens of companies that will do better over time than the best the U.S. has to offer. I believe that once you get beyond a short select list, you're compromising and "forcing" second-rate companies into the portfolio. As we've seen from the historic record, on a broad basis, foreign stocks have never added significant value. And when we look forward, I wonder what reason you might give to support the contention that foreign stocks will outperform U.S. companies in the future. In addition, I think the record is very clear on the reality that international diversification does little or nothing to cushion drastic market declines here in the U.S. As with small caps, I'm waiting for some solid *factual* evidence to convince me.

OBJECTION: What if the market crashes? You'll have all your money in the big stocks and will have nothing to cushion the decline!

ANSWER: There's only one place that is sure to cushion the effects of a market crash: cash. It is folly to think that you can allocate into other equity asset classes and hope they will protect you in a severe market decline. There is absolutely no evidence to suggest that this is possible. You can spread your money around as much as possible, but when the market tanks, it takes everything down with it. Sure, there may be some minor variations. Perhaps if large caps decline 28% you might find an asset class that only went down 24%, but that's scant comfort in tough times.

If you want to address your concern about a severe market decline, you'd be much better served to look at how much of your portfolio is in bonds and cash, rather than seek to hedge one equity asset class with another equity asset class. Hedging one equity risk with another equity may work on paper in an academic setting; I challenge you to show me how it has ever produced significant long-term value in a real world environment.

OBJECTION: So you're saying that large caps will always do better than small caps and foreign stocks?

ANSWER: Of course not. No single asset class can be the top performer all the time. I guarantee that there will be periods when the best performing funds are small cap or international. But while I'll admit that large-cap U.S. stock funds won't be the best *all the time*, I can make the case that it will be the best *over time*. And that's what really counts for the long-term buy-and-hold investor.

OBJECTION: So what happens when large-cap U.S. stock funds are not performing the best?

ANSWER: Relax. Where is it written that your portfolio needs to be hitting on all cylinders all the time? That's a most unrealistic expectation. As we've seen, it leads to hazardous short-term thinking. Of course, you could always spread your money out into so many asset classes that you'll always have *something* doing well in your portfolio. You'll also always have something doing poorly. The net result will be a portfolio that has been "drugged" to smooth out the short-term ups and downs—and produce long-term mediocrity. It's much wiser and more productive to learn how to control your short-term frustrations so that you don't commit long-term errors. The problem may not be with the markets, but with your expectations.

OBJECTION: But I hear that tech is overvalued. What if we get a big tech correction? Won't I lose a lot of money?

ANSWER: What do you mean, "What *if* we get..." The fact is we are *sure* to get a big tech correction. It happens almost every year. Sometimes even twice a year. Technology stocks are volatile, no question about it. Do you know how many times Intel and Microsoft have declined 15–25% over the past ten years? Trust me, you'd run out of fingers and toes counting. If you're going to invest in technology stocks you've got to remember that volatility is not the same as risk. The only time volatility is risky for the long-term investor is if you yourself make it so by panicking. Remember that you're investing in real companies, not just statistical listings on the stock pages. If the company and its prospects are still sound, the volatility should be seen for what it is: just a short-term manifestation of market neuroses.

OBJECTION: So you're saying that I should put all my money into Amazon.com and crazy Internet stocks?

ANSWER: This is the old straw man argument. A long-term strategy using growth funds with a technology emphasis is far different than speculating on just a few high flyers. Take the time to look at a typical growth fund portfolio. You'll see it filled with names like Intel, Lucent, Merck, Pfizer, GE, Microsoft, Time Warner, Cisco, and Citigroup. Far from speculative, this is in reality a *blue chip* strategy.

APPENDIX A

PERFORMANCE BACKGROUND

I generally take a pretty skeptical view of the motivations of those who claim that the "system" is messed up. Far too often we find that the source of their complaints is simply frustration that they have not been able to succeed within the structure of the current system. Rather than blame themselves, they point fingers at everything around them. I would expect that a book like this that takes issue with much of the conventional wisdom in the fund world might raise questions about what the results at Markman Capital have been. Accordingly, in the interest of full disclosure, we thought it only fair to write about the performance of portfolios managed by Markman Capital.

Since early 1995, Markman Capital has acted as the advisor to the Markman MultiFunds, three no-load funds of funds. These funds have public, audited records. The Aggressive Allocation Portfolio, the primarily equity-oriented long-term growth option is the fund that most closely parallels the objectives and risk level of the portfolios of *The New York Times* experts discussed in chapter five. From the beginning of 1995 through June 30, 1999, the performance comparisons were as follows:

Total Return Comparisons*

Markman Aggressive Allocation . . . .+144%

Jack Brill Portfolio . . . .+133%

Sheldon Jacobs Portfolio . . . .+124%

Eric Kobren Portfolio . . . .+123%

Morningstar Portfolio . . . .+105%

Harold Evensky Portfolio . . . .+ 84%

Annualized Return Comparisons*

Markman 23.4%

Brill 20.6%

Jacobs 19.6%

Kobren 19.5%

Morningstar 17.3%

Evensky 14.5%

*Note that the Markman numbers are net *after* the annual fee charged to the fund of .95%. No deductions for fees and expenses were made from the other portfolios. Also, the actual start date of the Markman Portfolio was 2/1/95. Since January of 1995 was a month of generally positive returns, that also gives the N.Y. Times participants a bit of extra advantage.

PERFORMANCE AGAINST OTHER FUNDS OF FUNDS

The returns for the Markman MultiFunds since inception have exceeded most other funds of funds. The Fund of Funds Association uses data from Lipper Analytical Services to rank the performance of funds of funds in three categories: Conservative, Moderate, and Growth. The categories were established based on degree of volatility compared to the S&P 500. Markman Capital Management is a founding member of the Funds of Funds Association. Past performance is not predictive of future performance. Here is how the three Markman Multi-Funds compare with the average in each of the categories:

Annualized Returns 2/1/95 – 6/30/99

Markman Aggressive Allocation 23.4%

Average Growth Fund of Funds 19.8%

Markman Moderate Allocation 18.9%

Average Moderate Fund of Funds 18.0%

Markman Conservative Allocation 14.4%

Average Conservative Fund of Funds 13.0%

MARKMAN PORTFOLIOS
VS. VANGUARD

Back in the days when I was still foolishly drinking from the cup of conventional wisdom, some of my comments caught the eye of John Bogle, then chairman of the Vanguard group of mutual funds. We briefly corresponded on the topic of managed mutual funds versus index funds. Bogle, of course, favored indexing while I, not surprisingly, championed trying to find those fund managers who could possibly beat the index. Additionally, Bogle looked with dismay at the 0.95% I charged on top of the fees for the underlying funds my portfolios owned. Such costs, he felt (and still does feel) must inevitably lead to underperformance. Ever the sportsman, Bogle wrote to propose a "little side bet that our Index Trust will outperform your Multifund Trust over, say, the next five years." Regrettably, I took the bait and made the bet. I compounded my error by suggesting that we compare his Index 500 Fund to my Moderate Allocation Portfolio. Big mistake, for two reasons. First I had no idea back in early 1995 that the S&P would go on a multi-year tear, trouncing just about every other investment option. Equally foolish was to agree to compare a portfolio that had a significant bond component (my fund) to the all stock S&P Index Fund.

Suffice it to say that as of this writing, while the time for the contest is not yet up, the race is pretty much over. I lost and it wasn't even close.

Nevertheless, I do believe that I *have* proved my point about the value of managed portfolios over indexing, as well as the wisdom of paying a fee for the right kind of advice. For when we construct a more realistic apples-to-apples comparison of The Markman Multifund to Vanguard's LifeStrategy Funds of Funds, we get a truer picture of how our different philosophies and strategies play out in the real world. The Vanguard Life Strategy Funds are blends of several of Vanguard's funds in multifund portfolios. Most of the funds used are index funds. The one exception is the Vanguard Asset Allocation Fund which, while not an index fund, still has the very low fees typical of Vanguard. Theirs is a fine product and I've often said that it is the benchmark of excellence against which all other funds of funds should measure themselves.

The performance results, after about 4.5 years, are as follows:

Annualized Returns 2/1/95 – 6/30/99

Markman Aggressive Allocation Fund 23.4%

Vanguard LifeStrategy Growth 21.4%

Markman Moderate Allocation Fund 18.9%

Vanguard LifeStrategy Moderate Growth 18.7%

Markman Conservative Allocation Fund 14.4%

Vanguard LifeStrategy Conservative Growth 15.5%

So as we approach the five-year anniversary of my bet with John Bogle, our managed, non-indexed variety of fund of funds is ahead on two scorecards and behind on one. Had an investor put an equal amount in all three, the Markman Funds would have generated a better overall return thus far. Will that persist indefinitely into the future? No one can say yea or nay with any certainty. But these are the facts as they stand now.

APPENDIX B

THE GOOD STUFF: AN INCOMPLETE LIST

Most of what is written and spoken about investments is nothing more than empty calories. You can read and listen day after day and not be any wiser. There are, of course, some notable exceptions. Since I'm regularly asked for advice in these areas, I thought I'd take this opportunity to share with you what I like, who I read, and who I make it a point to listen to. Inclusion in this list does not mean that these writers or strategists necessarily agree with *me*. They may, in fact, disagree with some of what I've written. They are included because I respect their work and think investors should be familiar with their positions. (By the way, lack of inclusion of any particular person, book, etc., does not necessarily mean that I don't think he/she/it worthwhile. It may just be a simple oversight on my part.)

One of the most remarkable investment books I've ever read has been David Dreman's *Contrarian Investment Strategies: The Next Generation*. Dreman is one of the deans of value investing and would probably cringe at my growth-oriented approach. Nevertheless, his book is full of wonderful insights about investing markets and individual investor psychology. Another extraordinary book is *Stocks for the Long Run* by Jeremy Siegel. This clearly written book provides a wealth of historical perspective and insights about how and why the markets do what they do. *Against*

The Gods by Peter Bernstein is a fascinating exploration of the history and nature of risk. Thomas Friedman's *The Lexus and the Olive Tree* will give you an entertaining and perceptive perspective on how the global economy is developing and impacting almost every area of endeavor. In *The Warren Buffet Portfolio*, fund manager Robert Hagstrom uses Buffet's example as a jumping off point to explore and argue for the virtues of a focused portfolio.

I try to avoid exposure to the market gurus and assorted investment strategists that parade hourly on CNBC and other media outlets. Most of them are so wrong so often that listening to them makes my teeth hurt. There are two notable exceptions: Abby Joseph Cohen and Joe Battipaglia. When you have an opportunity to hear these folks talk, it pays to listen.

- Abby Joseph Cohen is chief market strategist for Goldman Sachs and has, more than any other major analyst, correctly assessed the nature of this bull market. She has stood firm when others wavered and shown great vision when others were blinded by the smoke and dust thrown up by short-term market turbulence. She is truly the Xena, Warrior Princess, of the '90s bull market.

- Joe Battipaglia, chief market strategist for Gruntal & Co., is less of a household name. CNBC junkies will recognize him as a frequent guest on the Squawk Box program. Like Cohen, Battipaglia has been consistently right on the trend of this market. He has a tremendous grasp of how the pieces of our economy are fitting together and what impact that dynamic is having on the financial markets.

Of course, no strategist is always going to call it correctly. And there may well come a time when these two lose touch with what's really going on. But I do believe that Abby Joseph Cohen's and Joe Battipaglia's clear-headed vision and razor sharp intellectual rigor make them a good bet for some time to come.

Four other names in the investment world also come to mind when I think of people whose thoughts I always want to know.

◆ Ken Fisher is a money manager, author and columnist for *Forbes* magazine, and he does a great job in all three areas. His columns are alone worth the subscription to *Forbes*.

◆ Laszlo Birinyi also writes a column for *Forbes* and runs one of the best research shops in the country. Many of you will recognize him as a frequent panelist on Wall Street Week. You can always count on him for a bottom-line, baloney-free view of what's going on in the market.

◆ John Rekenthaler (whom you met earlier in our analysis of *The New York Times* fund-picking contest) is the research director of Morningstar. While he and I disagree on a few important topics, I find him to be one of the most intellectually honest people in the fund world. He is constantly expanding his vision (rare in our industry) and his analysis is probing and provocative.

◆ Another name associated with Morningstar is its CEO, Don Phillips. In an industry filled with oversized and unjustified egos shouting to be heard, Don brings a calm intelligence to everything he does and says. Again, I respectfully disagree with some of what he says (that doesn't mean he's wrong), but he is someone to whom you should pay attention.

There you have it. A list of the good stuff. Short, but with a lot of depth.

INDEX